My Faithbook Messages

Devotions to Like and Share

Sandra Fischer

Interior layout by Rachel Greene for elfinpen designs, http://elfinpen.com
Cover by Penoaks Publishing, http://penoaks.com
Published by Evergood Books
Southern Pines, NC
fishnet@islc.net

ISBN: 9780996838023

"like" button by Landan Lloyd from the Noun Project.
"comment" button by Jivan from the Noun Project.
"share" button by praveen patchu from the Noun Project.
"message" button by Xinh Studio from the Noun Project

To Faithwriters.com, the website that has provided me
the opportunity to publish and share my writings
along with thousands of other members
over a span of sixteen years.

Welcome to *My Faithbook Messages*

In our digitally driven world, many people search social media for messages that allow them to connect and interact with others, solve problems, or find advice. What if we investigate a source that has existed for centuries? I call it the *Faithbook*, a proven place to find answers, advice and hope. Yes, the book is the Bible, the ultimate social media resource of all time. It gives us the opportunity to interact with the Author (God), to find salvation in His Son (Jesus), and to receive daily advice from an all-knowing Counselor (Holy Spirit). We do not have to join an organization, nor depend on algorithms to view posts, nor wait until a page downloads; we have direct access to God's written Word.

It is in this *Faithbook,* the Bible, that I found verses that resonate with messages I want to share with you. I'm "posting" them on the pages that follow. As you explore these devotions, my prayer is that they will speak to you and encourage you as a believer in Christ. If you are not a Christian, I hope that as you read these devotions, you will discover how God sends messages to all of us and they might encourage you to visit His *Faithbook* and learn more about Him.

I present *My Faithbook Messages* in sixty "posts." Symbols to "Like" (👍), "Comment" (💬), and "Share" (↪) appear on each page. If you wish to "Like" or "Comment" on a message, share them by email to me: safischer37@gmail.com. If you wish to "Share" a devotion, simply follow the directions on page 124.

Some of the devotions came to me through ordinary means; others came by extraordinary ways. Each resounded with scriptures from the Bible that underscored them and made them distinct. Some messages are related to specific holidays or events. Others presented themselves via dramatic natural phenomena—when I witnessed the power of an electrical storm or the fierce winds of a hurricane. When I observed delicate, intricate flower blossoms or encountered fascinating creatures, I found missives about God's amazing creation. Perhaps the most meaningful messages came through my relationships and experiences with people viewed through the lenses of scripture.

Whenever the inspirations for these devotions came, I sensed God was revealing His faithful presence and significance in my life. The messages filtered through my mind and heart, into my hands and onto these pages. They became *My Faithbook Messages* that I joyfully share with you. May you be as blessed by them as I have been in posting them to you.

My Faithbook Messages

Devotions to Like and Share

HE HAS MADE
everything
beautiful
IN ITS TIME

~ ECCLESIASTES 3:11 ~

"From New Year to Eternity"

He has made everything beautiful in its time. Also, he has put eternity into man's heart.
~ Ecclesiastes 3:11a

Standing at an airport gate, one witnesses the many emotions of "hellos" and "goodbyes." We glow at joyful smiles of greeting and happy embraces for arrivals; we sadden at the long kisses and tearful hugs of those departing. *Life is hello. . .life is goodbye.* It's the constant tension of casting on and letting go. King Solomon noted this in the third chapter of Ecclesiastes: "For everything there is a season. . .a time to plant, and a time to pluck up. . .a time to embrace and a time to refrain." (v. 3:1, 2b, 5b)

As we turn the page to a new year, we have a choice—to greet it with hope and joy, letting go the past, or to keep standing at the gate hanging on to regrets. As Time begins to write in our New Year's blank book, let us look to embrace one word: *opportunity.* Let us seek it on days when clouds veil its appearance and let us greet it on days when it arrives skipping in the sunshine. Let us meet it as God's way of allowing us to discover all the possibilities it holds. Solomon recognizes God's offering to do his part when he says, "He has made everything beautiful in its time." (Ecclesiastes 3:11a) Talk about possibilities!

Somehow, as Time records our earthly journey, we sense there is a place of timelessness, a place of only "hellos," a place the wise King says God has put in our hearts, a place called eternity, our home in heaven forever as adopted children of God through Christ. Until then, we can appreciate all the prospects any passing moment offers as God-given.

How do you view the future? With anticipation, hope, or fear? How can placing your trust in God help you view it from His perspective?

To "Like" or "Comment" on this devotion or any that follow, email me: safischer37@gmail.com. To "Share" any devotion, go to page 124.

For His

LOVINGKINDNESS

Is

GREAT

toward us. . .

~ Psalm 117:2

"Of Love, Vines and Valentines"

For His lovingkindness is great toward us, And the truth of the LORD is everlasting. Praise the LORD!
~ Psalm 117:2 NASB

Have you ever noticed how mandevilla or clematis vines intertwine so tightly that the stems are indistinct from one another? Like the word "lovingkindness," which appears many times in the Book of Psalms, the compounding of these two benevolent actions make them truly inseparable. One cannot be sincerely kind without being loving, nor genuinely loving without being kind. Like the intertwining of the vines, the action of loving is inexorably intertwined with kindness.

Each year we celebrate Valentine's Day with its various expressions of love and kindness. The St. Valentine tradition of sending love messages is a good one, but I like what another saint named Augustine said:

"What does Love look like? It has hands to help others and feet to hasten to the poor and needy. It has eyes to see misery and want and ears to hear the sighs and sorrows of fellow men. That is what Love looks like."

In Augustine's view, love is manifested through our deepest sensitivity to others' needs, followed by putting that love into sacrificial action. This is lovingkindness. You can see it in those who aid victims of sudden natural disasters, such as wildfires, mudslides, and devastating hurricanes.

We see it in neighbors and friends reaching out to those suffering from a disabling disease, the loss of a loved one or other heartbreaks, those personal storms that overwhelm us. That's love and kindness intertwined.

God spread His lovingkindness abroad as an example of what our relationship should be with Him and others. We need Him. We need each other. We need lovingkindness. Perhaps that's why the Master Gardener "planted" the idea in the first place.

Do you know someone who shows lovingkindness? How will you show it to others?

Be truly
GLAD
There is wonderful
JOY
ahead
~1 Peter 1:6a

"Is There Such A Thing as Happily Ever After?"

So be truly glad. There is wonderful joy ahead...
~ 1 Peter 1:6a NLT

The Hallmark television channel is popular with many romanticists who spend hours watching the movies they air. Every movie's ending is predictable, implicit with the idea that the couple who kiss at the end will live happily ever after.

Is there such a thing? Yes and no. For us Christians, as members of God's family in His eternal kingdom, we have everlasting joy—good news—but not always experienced in the here and now on earth, not so good news. The second part of the verse quoted from 1 Peter ends with this reality check: "... even though you have to endure many trials for a little while." (1 Peter 1:6b NLT)

And Jesus tells His followers that trouble is a given: "In the world you will have tribulation." And then he follows with the good news, "... but take heart, I have overcome the world." (John 16:33b)

Paul's letter to Timothy has a similar promise for believers: "Indeed, all who desire to live a godly life in Christ Jesus will be persecuted...But as for you, continue in what you have learned and have firmly believed... the Sacred Writings, which are able to make you wise for salvation through faith in Christ Jesus." (2 Timothy 3:12, 14a, 15b)

For Christians, our earthly journey is underscored with everlasting joy in the hereafter. For those who have not accepted Christ's gift of salvation, there is no "happily ever after" beyond this world. "For God so loved the world, that he gave his only Son, that whoever believes in him should not perish but have eternal life. For God did not send his Son into the world to condemn the world, but in order that the world might be saved through him." (John 3:16-17)

Have you learned that happiness ever after is dependent on a relationship with Jesus and salvation through faith in Him?

Special Note: If you are not sure about where you will spend eternity, please visit this website for more information: www.peacewithGod.net

"Love Letters"

You yourselves are our letter of recommendation, written on our hearts, to be known and read by all. And you show that you are a letter from Christ delivered by us, written not with ink but with the Spirit of the living God, not on tablets of stone but on tablets of human hearts.
~ 2 Corinthians 3:2-3

Love letters have changed. Once written by hand on fine stationery, now they come in all kinds of digital forms. But one kind of love letter will never go out of style. It's the one Paul spoke about in his epistle to the Corinthians. "You yourselves are our letter. . .from Christ. . .written not with ink but with the Spirit of the living God."

All people are "letters" of some kind, conveying "messages" to others, expressed in words and deeds. As Christians we are letters too. What do others "read" from our speech and behavior? Do they see us as "love letters" of Christ or something not befitting the love He gave for all people? When we lay claim to Christ, we are making ourselves "known and read by all" as His representatives. "We are ambassadors for Christ, God making his appeal through us." (2 Corinthians 5:20)

As God's "living letters," He is using us to appeal to those who do not know Him, so they will want to know Him too. He's also appealing to other believers to see Christ's love living in us, an encouragement in their journey of faith. If we show the love of Christ through the overflow of the Spirit inked in our hearts, we will be "living love letters" to everyone we meet.

Has someone ever been a "love letter" of Christ to you? How can you show what the Spirit has inked on your heart to someone today?

Delight yourself

In the *LORD*

and

He will give you

the desires of your

~Psalm 37:4

"Getting our Heart's Desire"

Delight yourself in the LORD, and He will give you the desires of your heart.
~ Psalm 37:4

When we put coins in a vending machine, select a product and receive the one we choose, we are satisfied with the transaction. Our expectations are met. The motive behind our actions is the fulfillment of our desire because of what we gave to get it fulfilled.

Perhaps we get the same idea when we read Psalm 37:4. It may seem as if, when we praise God and delight in Him, He will give us whatever *we* want. Do we believe it to mean that *our* prayers and *our* wants are going to be fulfilled in exchange for our simply delighting in Him? Sounds reasonable (and delightful), but we should think about it. Are we treating His promises and blessings as vending machine products, dispensed to us because we earned them?

The promise for us to receive our heart's desire is based on the object of our delight. If it is for the LORD Himself, will He not give Himself to us? What greater delight could there be? As the psalmist wrote, "The Lord is my chosen portion and my cup." (Psalm 16:5a) and as He tells us in Psalm 23, our cup overflows with Him (v.5).

God does promise to give us the desires of our heart when we delight in Him. We find joy in His presence and fulfillment beyond measure as we exalt in Him for who He is, our LORD and our delight.

Do you "delight" in God and take joy in knowing Him as your loving heavenly Father? Tell Him.

Unless the LORD builds the house, those who build it labor in vain.

~ Psalm 127:1

"A Building of God"

Unless the LORD builds the house, those who build it labor in vain
~ Psalm 127:1a

After retirement, we moved to a new community and built a new house. When the foundation and framework appeared, I saw a blessing from God that I wanted to acknowledge. Using a marker, I inscribed cement bases and wood studs with Bible verses:

- Doorpost—*As for me and my house, we will serve the LORD.* (Joshua 24:15c)
- Living Room—Show *hospitality.* (Romans 12:13)
- Kitchen—*Give us this day our daily bread.* (Matthew 6:11)
- Pantry—*My food is to do the will of the one who sent me.* (John 4:34)
- Dining Room—*Taste and see that the LORD is good.* (Psalm 34:8a)
- Laundry Room—*If we confess our sins, He is faithful and just and will forgive us our sins and purify us from all unrighteousness.* (1 John 1:9)
- Sunroom—*The sun of righteousness will rise with healing in his wings.* (Malachi 4:2)
- Bedrooms—*Come to me, all you who labor and are heavy laden, and I will give you rest.* (Matthew 11:28)
- Baths—*Wash me, and I shall be whiter than snow.* (Psalm 51:7b)
- Stairway—*Let us . . .keep in step with the Spirit.* (Galatians 5:25)
- Study—*Blessed is the one who finds wisdom, and the one who gets understanding.* (Proverbs 3:13)

After the house was finished, I kept a copy of the verses tucked in my Bible. When I re-read them, I am overcome with gratitude for the home God provided. More so, I am grateful for the house He is building in me through the construction of the Holy Spirit and the room He has reserved for me in a heavenly mansion.

Can you think of verses that show God's oversight where you reside?

Know that the LORD,

HE IS GOD!

It is he who made us,

and we are his;

we are his people,

and the sheep

of his pasture

~PSALM 100:3

"All God's Children"

Know that the Lord, He is God; It is He who has made us, and not we ourselves; We are His people and the sheep of His pasture.
~ Psalm 100:3 NKJV

Our granddaughter, Addie Grace, is a special needs child. When our daughter takes her out in public in a special stroller-wheelchair, she receives many questions about Addie's condition.

In one encounter a curious little girl asked, "What's wrong with her?" Our daughter answered that God had created her the way she is. The small inquisitor posed a new question, "Can she walk or talk?"

Our daughter explained, "She can walk, but she can't talk."

The little girl remarked, "She's beautiful, but I feel sorry for her."

Our daughter assured her, "Don't be sorry. God made her and loves her as much as He loves you."

This prompted the deeper question many people think but are reluctant to ask, "*Why* did God make her that way?"

"That's an exceptionally good question. Sometimes we don't know God's reasons, but we trust Him because He's God."

With wisdom only God can give, the little girl reflected, then said, "Maybe it's so I don't have to feel sorry for myself, because I can walk and talk."

Fighting tears, our daughter told her, "That's a good answer."

It's true. The LORD is God, and He has made us and not we ourselves. His ways and purposes are sometimes beyond our comprehension, but we can trust Him and thank Him for His providence in creating all His children.

Have you learned something from God's providence through others?

> The Lord gave
> and
> the Lord has taken away;
> blessed be
> the name of the Lord
>
> ~ Job 1:21b

"Peace Amidst Losses"

The Lord gave, and the Lord has taken away; blessed be the name
of the Lord.
~Job 1:21b

A friend of mine shared the losses in her life that seemed to come in droves. Her husband died of a slow, debilitating disease; a few months later her mother died. Now, just a few weeks from that, she is caring for her aging father who has deteriorating health. She said, "Despite the losses, I sense a peace God is giving me." I thought of Job. He acknowledged God's sovereignty amidst his losses: "Naked I came from my mother's womb, and naked shall I return. The Lord gave, and the Lord has taken away; blessed be the name of the Lord." (Job 1:21)

While we cannot understand God's ways, we do know that losses, including the death of loved ones, are a reality we face. How do we sense peace, like my friend has, when that reality comes? We can trust our faithful, sovereign God, who is over all life circumstances and say, like Job, "I know that my Redeemer lives." (Job 19:25a)

We have another example far more compelling than Job: Jesus. He suffered and died so we might have peace with God through His death and resurrection. And He gives us this ultimate promise, "In this world you will have tribulation, but take heart; I have overcome the world." (John 16:33b) With one hand, God took Jesus from the world, and with the other He sent His Holy Spirit to indwell Christ followers, to seal us as His children, fill us with His power, comfort us and give us peace.

How have you managed the losses you've experienced? How can you allow God to give you comfort and peace?

We belong to
a
spiritual
family tree
in Christ

"Our Spiritual Family Tree"

The apostle Paul wrote to the church at Corinth, I became your father in Christ Jesus through the gospel. . .be imitators of me.
~ 1 Corinthians 4:15b–16b

Do you have inherited features from someone in your biological family tree? I do. I have my "mother's eyes," my "father's red hair," and my "grandmother's pear-shaped physique." I also have features from people in what I call my "spiritual family tree." I have diligence to study God's Word instilled by a dedicated Sunday school teacher. I possess a hunger for righteousness from passionate pastors who preach God's truth. I bear a desire to serve others inspired by faithful church servants I know. Overall, as a child of God, I contain the constant guidance, comfort, and discernment of the Holy Spirit at work in me.

Paul emphasized the importance of nurturing faith in others. He called Timothy his "true child in the faith." (1 Timothy 1:2a) Paul could count innumerable others as part of his faith family—early believers who first read his letters and millions of us who still do. Can you point to people who are similar progenitors of your faith, members of your "spiritual family tree?"

At the top of every believer's family tree is God, our Father. "God decided in advance to adopt us into his own family by bringing us to himself through Jesus Christ." (Ephesians 1:5a NLT) And Jesus acknowledges our identity with Him, "For whoever does the will of God, he is my brother and sister and mother." (Mark 3:35)

Why not draw up a spiritual family tree of those who fostered your faith in Christ? If it includes people still living, tell them what they mean to you as your spiritual forebearers.

Who is in your spiritual family tree for whom you can be grateful? How can you be a member of someone else's tree by sharing your faith?

MAN DOES NOT LIVE BY
BREAD ALONE ~

"Food for a Starving World"

Do not work for food that perishes, but for the food that endures to eternal life, which the Son of Man will give you.
~John 6:27a

Many of us remember the words our mothers used to compel us as children to clean our dinner plates: "Starving children all over the world would be happy to have what's on your plate." It's true, but some of us stubborn children didn't "bite" and the food went to waste. Some of us retorted, "O.K. Send the food to them."

People in the world are starving for a different kind of food—spiritual nourishment from God's Word. After a forty day fast, Jesus was tempted by the devil to turn stones into bread. He quoted scripture, "Man shall not live by bread alone, but by every word that comes from the mouth of God." (Deuteronomy 8:3b)

Jesus commanded His followers to feed the hungry and to share Himself, the Bread of Life, by going into all the world sharing the gospel. The amount Americans give to missions is 6.4% of the total they give to all Christian causes, the same amount they spend on dieting programs[1]. How ironic!

What if we took the children's suggestion to their mothers about wasted food and gave food for both body and soul? What if we packed up our extra Bibles or purchased some to give to mission groups for distribution along with food and clothing? Or what if we included small Bibles in bags we give to the homeless in addition to food, or included them with food baskets given out at food banks?

Yes, we need to feed hungry bodies first, but not to the exclusion of giving them eternal food—the saving gospel of Jesus Christ.

How do you share your blessings with others, both material and those of your faith? Who can you share with today?

---

1 Weller, B. (2020, July 29). A World on Missions Statistics. Retrieved from https://messagemissions.com/mission-statistics/

I will NEVER leave you or forsake you ~

Hebrews 13:5b

"A Shelter in the Storms of Life"

. . . He has said, "I will never leave you nor forsake you."
~Hebrews 13:5b

When I lived in Indiana, tornadoes were a regular summer occurrence; in North Carolina, where I live now, hurricanes visit us occasionally. I think about how other storms—emotional, physical, and spiritual—come into our lives. Some, like tornadoes, are sudden and unpredictable; others, like hurricanes, give us time to prepare.

Regardless of the storms we experience, scripture tells us of their certainty. Jesus said, "In this world you will have tribulation. . ." (John 16:33a NKJV) He didn't say "might" or "could," the key word is "will." He finishes with words asking us to have a paradoxical attitude: ". . .but be of good cheer. . ." If He stopped there, we might ask, "Say, what?" But then, He underscores why we can accept assured tribulation; He says, "I have overcome the world." (John 16:33b)

When we consider the pain and destruction storms bring, we struggle with being "of good cheer" amidst them. It's a matter of focus. We need to realize, as Peter did when he walked on stormy water. If we take our eyes off Jesus, our faith falters, and we slip into the roiling waters of doubt. Even so, Jesus is there to lift us up and keep us safe.

No matter the storm, we believers in Christ can rest assured that Jesus was with us before the storm, is with us in the storm and will be with us when it's over. We have a strong shelter, the Rock of Ages on whom we stand. We can sing the old hymn that says it well: "Oh, Jesus is the Rock in a weary land, a shelter in the time of storm."

How can we refocus our attention to the LORD when we are in the middle of troubles? How can God's Word and praying help?

Train
Yourself
in
Godliness

TRAINING MANUAL

"Godliness Training at the Sanctification Spa"

...train yourself for godliness; for while bodily training is of some value, godliness is of value in every way, as it holds promise for the present life and also for the life to come.
~ 1 Timothy 4:7b-8

The apostle Paul wrote Timothy about the superiority of godliness training. Here are ideas for such training at the Holy Spirit's "Sanctification Spa:"

- <u>Warm-up</u> by breathing in each morning as you awake in gratitude to God.
- <u>Apply the balm</u> of God's promises, getting that "faithlift," which smooths out any wrinkles of doubt and fear facing you.
- <u>Exercise</u> your mind by doing five reps of memorizing a scripture three times a day.
- <u>Walk</u> in step with the Spirit to build up your faith stamina.
- <u>Run</u> to God when you need comfort or help.
- <u>Crunch</u> the temptation to sin.
- <u>Jog</u> your memory by recalling the times God has blessed you.
- <u>Stretch</u> your spiritual muscles by reading or studying the Bible.
- <u>Pull-up</u> to the curb at church each week to join in worship and Christian fellowship.
- <u>Sit-up</u> and take notice during sermons and Sunday school lessons to tone flabby faith.
- <u>Jump</u> at the chance to share the gospel of Jesus Christ whenever and wherever the opportunity arises.
- <u>Bend</u> your knees and your heart in prayer often.
- <u>Chin-up</u> when trials come by trusting God's providence.
- <u>Workout</u> your salvation daily as God works in you to shape you into Christ's image.

Training also includes subscribing to a good diet—feeding on the Bread of Life, drinking the Living Water and being the Salt of the Earth to the world.

Do you need more time at the "Sanctification Spa"? Is your faith getting flabby or are you toning up each day?

Where your
treasure is
there your
❤
will be also
~ Matthew 6:21

"Designer Purses and Heavenly Treasure"

...lay up for yourselves treasures in heaven, where neither moth nor rust destroys and where thieves do not break in and steal.
~ Matthew 6:20

Recently I was fascinated by one of the prizes offered on a game show—a collection of five designer purses valued at over $3,000. I personally do not know a woman who owns a purse costing even $600. If I did, she probably would have a significant amount of cash to carry in it too. But no matter whether a woman's purse is her treasure, or what money she puts into it, neither will last in the long run. The purse will wear out and the money will be spent or left to someone else to spend.

Some treasures can last forever, according to the words of Jesus to his disciples: "Provide yourselves with moneybags that do not grow old, with a treasure in the heavens that does not fail, where no thief approaches and no moth destroys." (Luke 12:33b)

We won't be carrying any purses into heaven, but we can store up deeds of grace and mercy by using our resources to "give to the needy" or by sharing the gospel as Jesus directs. The evidence will not be a designer name on what we do but a revelation of the imprint of Christ's rich love in our hearts: "For where your treasure is, there will your heart be also." (Matthew 6:21)

Where is your treasure kept? Where is your lasting, forever treasure and how can you share it?

WATCH AND PRAY

SO YOU WILL NOT

F

A

L

L

INTO TEMPTATION

~ MATTHEW 26:41

"The Wringer of Temptation"

Watch and pray so that you may not enter into temptation. The spirit indeed is willing, but the flesh is weak.
~Matthew 26:41

Washday was a big production at our home when I grew up in the 1940's and I was obliged to help. We had a double-tub electric machine with a wringer attachment. It had two wooden rollers that moved in opposite directions; they compressed the clothes inserted between them, squeezing out the water as they passed through. Operating it took careful finesse; clothing had to be folded and flattened out to start it through the rollers. The tricky part was pulling back fingers so they wouldn't go through too. There was a release lever to stop the rollers and spread them apart should a wad of clothing or part of a person get caught in the wringer.

I used that release button many times during my work as "laundry mistress." That wringer sucked my arm up to the elbow once before I could hit the release, and I was almost scalped when my long curls were caught.

I learned to have a healthy respect for that wringer. As I reflect on it, I liken it to the temptation to sin. Those moving rollers of temptation are waiting to clamp onto me and suck me in and it often happens when I'm trying to clean up my act. It can be my fleshly nature yielding to the world's enticements; I think I can pull myself back before I am entrapped.

Sometimes I end up to my elbows in its grasp. The release lever is the way out, the same one God provides us. The apostle Paul wrote: "No temptation has overtaken you that is not common to man. God is faithful, and he will not let you be tempted beyond your ability, but with the temptation he will also provide the way of escape, that you may be able to endure it." (1 Corinthians 10:13) God provides the release lever, the way out, but I must push it, so I won't be caught by the wringer of temptation.

How do you deal with temptations that come in your life? How can knowing God is present help you?

In your hearts honor

CHRIST *the* **LORD**
as holy, always being prepared
to
make a defense for the
HOPE
that is in you;
yet do it with gentleness and respect.

~ 1 Peter 3:15

30

"Believers Pop Quizzes"

But in your hearts honor Christ the Lord as holy, always being prepared to make a defense to everyone who asks you to give the reason for the hope that is in you.
~ 1 Peter 3:15a

Most students have had teachers who gave "pop" quizzes: those dreaded, unexpected tests to determine if they were absorbing what was taught and were able to prove it by passing the tests. In Peter's first letter to early believers, he forewarned them to expect to have their faith tested by those who wanted to know about the hope they had in Christ.

He knew that their love of Christ would arouse curiosity in non-believers. As true disciples, they would be "quizzed" about why they revere Jesus. He cautioned them to "always be prepared" for such "pop quizzes." That wise advice hasn't changed over the years. As followers of Christ, each of us must be prepared to share the gospel with everyone who asks.

How do we prepare for those encounters? We have the Holy Spirit power that was given believers as told in Acts 1:8a: "But you will receive power when the Holy Spirit comes upon you, and you will be my witnesses." And, by that power, we should be willing to share how Jesus took our sin upon the cross, died, was buried, and rose again to give us eternal life.

Are you ready for any "Believers Pop Quizzes" that may come your way? Pray as Paul did: "Pray. . . that whenever I speak, words may be given me so that I will fearlessly make known the mystery of the gospel." (Ephesians 6:19 NIV) If so prepared, we can ace those "pop quizzes!"

How can you be prepared to share the gospel when others quiz you about your faith? How can your personal testimony be a way to show how God has impacted your life?

Blessed are
those
who hear
the word of
God
and keep it
~ Luke 11:28

"Are you Talking to Me?"

Blessed are those who hear the word of God and keep it.
~Luke 11:28

Have you ever listened to a convicting sermon and thought, "So and so (fill in the name) should hear this?" Or have you received a devotional or Bible verse by email or text feed that spoke to a behavior you wish someone else would change? Do you hit forward so they will get the message? I've done that, thinking to encourage someone's spiritual maturity—until one day a faithful friend asked me, "Do you think maybe God might be speaking to you?"

My first thought was defensive, but the Holy Spirit convicted me to examine myself. Was I the one God wanted the message to reach and, by thinking God had someone else in mind, was I being self-righteous and hypocritical? The words of an old hymn came to mind: "It's me, it's me, it's me, oh, Lord, standing in the need of prayer; not my brother, not my sister, but me."

I also remembered the admonition in Matthew 7:3-5 (NIV): "Why do you look at the speck of sawdust in your brother's eye and pay no attention to the plank in your own eye? How can you say to your brother, 'Let me take the speck out of your eye,' when all the time there is a plank in your own eye? You hypocrite, first take the plank out of your own eye, and then you will see clearly to remove the speck from your brother's eye."

So, I prayed, asking for forgiveness and for discernment about messages God means for me and not necessarily for someone else.

Have you ever misconstrued a message you thought was for someone else and not you? How can we be open to receiving what God means for us?

Easter Clothes

Robed in

His Righteousness

"Dressed in Easter Best"

But when the king came in to look at the guests, he saw there a man who
had no wedding garment.
~ Matthew 22:11

Where I grew up, everyone donned their Sunday best attire for Easter. Men sported new suits. Women boasted the latest spring fashions, crowned with hats adorned in flowers and ribbons. Young girls wore white or pastel bonnets, lacy socks, and patent leather shoes.

I recalled this when reading the parable of the wedding feast given by the king (God) for his son (Jesus) in Matthew 22. The guests needed to be clothed in proper wedding garments, or they were unacceptable. When one of them appeared improperly dressed, the king threw him out.

True Easter apparel is not found in fashionable suits, dresses, and bonnets. Real Easter attire was provided on a cross draped with Jesus, whose death and resurrection offered the means for all to come to the future wedding feast in heaven. The parable in Matthew is a warning to those not clothed for that future event in the proper attire—the righteousness of Christ.

What have you chosen to wear for Easter? Will you be dressed properly, able to sing the words of the hymn, "And Can It Be?"

No condemnation now I dread;
Jesus, and all in Him, is mine!
Alive in Him, my living Head,
And clothed in righteousness Divine,
Bold I approach the eternal throne,
And claim the crown, through Christ my own.

What Easter clothes are you wearing for heaven's wedding feast?

Blessed are those
. . .who seek him with
their whole heart

~Psalm 119:2

"Healer of Our Hearts"

Blessed are those who keep his testimonies, who seek him with their whole heart.
~Psalm 119:2

Our first granddaughter was born with a hole in her heart. The prognosis was that she would need surgery to close the hole unless it closed on its own. God answered our prayers to heal it without surgery and she is a healthy young adult today.

Pascal, a 17th century theologian, contended that all of us are born with spiritual holes in our hearts. He said this God-shaped vacuum in the heart of every person does not heal on its own and cannot be filled by any created thing. Only God can fill it.

Some of us try to fill it with people or things—family, friends, jobs, hobbies, achievements, or material possessions. Some even use drugs or other addictive substances to fill the void. We search what the world offers to make us complete, but only Jesus can fill that empty space, if we allow Him to do so. Only Christ, the heart healer, can close the hole in our hearts and make us whole.

Has the hole in your heart been healed? Or are you searching for someone or something to fill it? The answer is just a prayer away. Ask God to forgive your sin and accept His gift of grace through Christ's provision by His death, burial, and resurrection.

Here is the heart-healing promise in Romans 10:9-10: . . ."because, if you confess with your mouth that Jesus is Lord and believe in your heart that God raised him from the dead, you will be saved. For with the heart one believes and is justified, and with the mouth one confesses and is saved."

Does your heart have a hole in it? Do you know who can heal it? Will you allow Him to do so? If you are unsure, visit www.peacewithGod.net

Pursue

Righteousness

Faith
Love
and

Peace

"Great Expectations"

Jesus said to them, "You don't know what you are asking."
~Mark 10:38a

Has anyone ever asked something of you with preconceived expectations and hidden motives? According to Mark's gospel, James and John did exactly that when they told Jesus: "Teacher, we want you to do for us whatever we ask of you." (Mark 10:35b) Such audacity might elicit a sharp rebuttal by almost anyone—except Jesus, who simply asked what they wanted. Their answer revealed hidden, selfish motives.

They wanted Jesus to grant them positions of honor, to sit at His right and left in His glory. "You don't know what you are asking," he explained. (v.38) To follow His course would mean a way of suffering and death. He added, "to sit at my right hand or my left is not mine to grant." (v.40) Perhaps their recent experience of being part of Jesus' inner circle at the Transfiguration prompted them to presume upon Jesus.

I wonder if we presume upon God sometimes when we pray. Do we have great expectations for Him to "do for us whatever we ask?" And, like James and John, do we know what granting our prayers might mean for us?

Scripture does tell us that we can ask anything in prayer, but we should not presume upon God with wrong motives. James writes, "you do not receive [answers to prayers], because you ask with wrong motives." (James 4:3a NIV) And Paul exhorts us to "call on the LORD from a pure heart." (2 Timothy 2:22b)

Jesus taught us to pray to the Father for His will to be done. He will meet that expectation every time.

How can we pray for God's will by surrendering our own? How does humility honor God?

What's in your cup?

The good person out of his good treasure brings forth good. . .

~ Matthew 12:35

"What's in your Cup?"

The good person out of his good treasure brings forth good, and the evil person out of his evil treasure brings forth evil.
~ Matthew 12:35

A story circulated on social media about someone who is accidentally jostled by another person while holding a cup of coffee, causing a spill and consternation at themselves or at the jostler. What we can learn from this event is not about what or who caused the spill, but instead what is relevant is what the cup contains. Whatever is in our "cup," or in our hearts, will spill out when we are bumped. When you are shaken by any of life's circumstances, what spills out of your cup? Gratitude or grumbling? Grace or greed? Service or selfishness? Faith or fear? Worship or worry? Prayer or panic?

We see the best and worst spilling out of people when a disaster or crisis shakes them. Schemers, hoarders, and scammers abound by taking advantage of the situation for personal gain. Others, whether by vocation or resolve, reach out to help in any way possible, some even giving their lives by putting themselves in harm's way.

Christians are to be filled in this way: ". . . with the Spirit, speaking to one another in psalms and hymns and spiritual songs, singing and making melody with your heart to the Lord; always giving thanks for all things in the name of our Lord Jesus Christ to God, even the Father." (Ephesians 5:18b-20a NASB)

When our cup is filled with the Spirit, goodness, mercy, and grace will overflow, running over, despite what sudden circumstances shake us.

What spills out from you when something or someone "shakes" you up? How can we be filled with the Spirit, so what "spills" out of us will be a blessing?

So also faith by itself, if it does not have works, is dead.

James 2:17

"Tell and Show"

So also faith by itself, if it does not have works, is dead.
~ James 2:17

Most writers who want to improve their skill are advised to use words that "show" their story rather than ones that merely "tell" it. While faith is the root of salvation, works are the fruit of it. The works or fruit are our actions, what we "show" as proof of what we "tell" about our faith. "What is it, my brothers, if someone says he has faith but does not have works? . . .if a brother or sister is poorly clothed and lacking in daily food, and one of you says to them, 'Go in peace, be warmed and filled,' without giving them the things needed for the body, what good is that? So, also faith by itself if it does not have works, is dead." (James 2:14-17)

Our behavior displays what we say we believe. While faith is the root of salvation, works are the fruit of it, the proof that what we "tell" we are "showing" in what we do. Lip service comes easy for all of us, but putting our hearts and hands to act out what we say gives life to our words. D.L. Moody said the Bible should be bound in shoe leather, putting feet to our faith.

As believers, we know we are saved by faith, a gift of God, but it becomes a working faith when we unwrap it to show it is not faith *by* works, but faith *that* works—a faith that reveals Christ in us, the hope of glory. Someone has said the best sermons given are those that, if necessary, use words. We are called to "tell" *and* "show" the gospel.

How does what you show about your faith in Christ line up with what you say about it?

> *The LORD is good to those who wait for him, to the soul who seeks him*
>
> Lamentations 3:25

"Growing Patience"

The Lord is good to those who wait for him, to the soul who seeks him.
~Lamentations 3:25

In our fast-paced culture, we have developed an insatiable need for instant gratification. We want information, service, and products and we want them now! Patience is a Christian virtue signifying spiritual maturity, fruit produced by the Spirit in us.

A word search in scripture for "wait" or its synonyms produces anywhere from 106 to 396 instances. The LORD has a purpose when He wants us to "wait," and He gives examples of people who learned that purpose. Abraham waited decades for the heir God promised—although he and Sarah tried their own "hurry-up" method. Jacob worked an extra seven years to claim Rachel as his wife. Joseph languished in prison over a decade, waiting for God to fulfill the dreams given him, and when we say someone has "the patience of Job," we remember his endurance in suffering.

So, what does God want us to learn about waiting? The bottom line is—to trust Him to fulfill *His* plan and purpose in *His* timing. "He hath made every thing beautiful in His time." (Ecclesiastes 3:11a KJV) God will nurture us in the same way He does a fruit-bearing tree as it goes through the long process of growing fruit.

If we depend upon God, our spiritual source of nourishment—through prayer and feeding on His Word—He will transform us from young, weak seedlings into strong, productive fruit-bearers. We do well to allow the Spirit to work in us while we wait. As the psalmist says, "Wait on the Lord; Be of good courage, And He shall strengthen your heart; Wait, I say, on the Lord!" (Psalm 27:14 NKJV)

How patient are you in everyday circumstances while waiting for God to answer prayer or to fulfill His promises and purposes? How can we learn to be more patient?

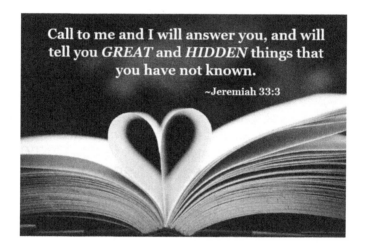

Call to me and I will answer you, and will tell you *GREAT* and *HIDDEN* things that you have not known.

~Jeremiah 33:3

"Heavenly Live Chat Room – Always Open"

And this is the confidence that we have toward Him: that if we ask anything according to his will he hears us.
~ 1 John 5:14

When I used an online "live chat" feature with a person about a need I had with his company, the process made me think. As I typed in my question, the word "listening" appeared by the online helper's name. When he wrote an answer to me, the word "responding" appeared. At the end of the "chat," the helper wrote, "Is there anything else you need?"

I thought about how this relates to prayer. Each day we have an opportunity to have a "live chat" at any time with our heavenly Father. He promises in Jeremiah 29:12 that we can be assured He is listening: "'Then you will call upon me and come and pray to me, and I will hear you."

He also promises He will respond in Jeremiah 33:3: "Call to me and I will answer you, and will tell you great and hidden things that you have not known."

And, just like the company helper in the "live chat," He assures us He is ready to provide our very need in Christ as promised in Philippians 4:19: "And my God will supply every need of yours according to his riches in glory in Christ Jesus."

Have you had a "live chat" with God today? He's always "online" and available. He listens. He responds. He offers to supply our every need.

How are your "live chats" with God going? How comforting is it to know He is always ready and wanting to chat with us?

BUT HE GIVES US MORE GRACE.
THAT IS WHY SCRIPTURE SAYS:

"God opposes the proud but shows favor to the humble."

James 4:6

"Learning about Grace"

But he gives us more grace. That is why Scripture says: 'God opposes the proud but shows favor to the humble.'
~James 4:6 NIV

Our granddaughter's middle name is Grace, given to her at birth. She was born with many handicaps; it appeared to some that Grace may not have been an appropriate name. She possesses a rare genetic deletion causing her to be virtually deaf, mentally slow, and developmentally challenged, but she has lived up to her name by demonstrating its meaning to those who know her. She has blessed so many of our lives by showing us the nature of Christ in her unspoken ways.

She does not talk back to her parents, nor say unkind things to anyone. She doesn't roll her eyes or sigh in judging others' appearances or demeanor. She never lies nor gossips and does not make promises she cannot keep. She does not hold grudges and is never hypocritical. She delights in simple things and is not enamored by riches, fame, or worldly pursuits.

While devoid of some abilities given to others, God has given her the gift of showing us the attributes of grace, a humble example all of us can take to heart by displaying such considerations in our own speech and actions. I am so grateful to God for giving us more grace through our own dear Addie Grace.

Has God shown His grace to you through the life of someone else?

"Me, Myself and the 'Other Guy'"

Lord, what about him?
~ John 21:21b NIV

Ever find yourself concerned about what someone else has or is getting in life compared with you? You may be teetering on the sin of covetousness. Many of us are familiar with the "greener grass" temptation we view on the "other side of the fence," leading us to compare our lives with other people.

Peter did it. In chapter 21 of John, Jesus tells Peter three times to care for the "sheep," His followers. Jesus indicates the kind of death Peter would experience, ending with an emphatic, "Follow me!" Instead of focusing on Jesus' command, Peter turns to look at John and asks, "Lord, what about him?" He's concerned with what Jesus had in mind for the "other guy." Jesus said, "If I want him to remain alive until I return, what is that to you? You must follow me." (John 21:22 NIV)

God has a plan and purpose for each of us—to focus on Him, to follow where He leads us, and to remain faithful to His specific plan and purpose for us. When we begin to wonder about the "other guy" and what God has in mind for him or her, we need to heed the voice of Jesus saying to us, "What is that to you? You must follow me." From Peter's response after Jesus spoke this to him, we can see that he did refocus and follow Jesus. He trusted his life and death to Christ, faithfully serving and glorifying Him. We can do no less. Our Shepherd calls each of us as individuals. "...He calls his own sheep by name and leads them out." (John 10:3b NIV.) Let's focus on our own path, following Him.

Do you compare yourself or what you have with others? How can we learn to be content with what God has in mind for us?

Do not be anxious about ANYTHING, but in EVERYTHING by PRAYER and SUPPLICATION with THANKSGIVING let your requests be made known to GOD

~ PHILIPPIANS 4:6-7

"Two Spreading Viruses"

*Do not be anxious about anything, but in everything, by prayer and
supplication, with thanksgiving, let your requests be made known to
God. And the peace of God, which surpasses all understanding, will guard
your hearts and your minds in Christ Jesus.*
~ Philippians 4:6-7

A disabling, contagious virus is spreading throughout the world, causing
great harm to people. Its name is "anxiety," and it is exhibited by fear and
panic. It's a "companion" to any flu or coronavirus that causes illness and
death in its wake. As Christians we should do what we can to protect
ourselves against the threat of both.

Paul exhorts us in his Philippian letter to be anxious about nothing, and
there are hundreds of scriptures admonishing us to "fear not." This does
not mean we should mindlessly dismiss threats to our safety or well-
being. In fact, the Greek word "merimnah" used in this verse is translated
two ways in the New Testament—one negatively, another positively. It
means "worry" or "anxiety" when used in a negative sense, as when Jesus
says, "Do not 'worry' about your life. . ." (Matthew 6:25a NIV) When used
in a positive way, it is translated as "concern" in Paul's letter to the
Corinthians, ". . . so that there should be no division in the body, but that
its parts should have equal 'concern' [merimnah] for each other."
(1 Corinthians 12:25 NIV)

Worry or anxiety dwells on "what ifs" or future unknowns. Concern
conveys positive aspects, focusing on a problem in a beneficial way. We
should take measures to protect ourselves from a threatening viral disease
and, if we trust God for things beyond our control, we will protect
ourselves from the "anxiety" virus too. Prayer is essential in dealing with
both.

**How do you handle feelings of anxiety when they occur? What measures
can you take to help you trust God no matter the circumstances?**

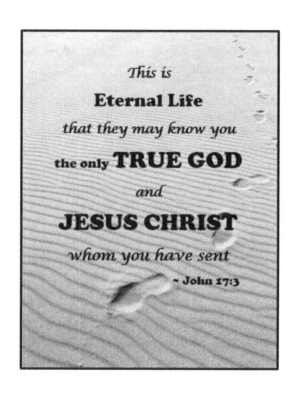

This is
Eternal Life
that they may know you
the only **TRUE GOD**
and
JESUS CHRIST
whom you have sent
~ John 17:3

"The Beginning of the End?"

And this is eternal life, that they know you, the only true God, and Jesus Christ whom you have sent.
~John 17:3

When a natural disaster occurs or a widespread virus sweeps the world, people begin to ask, "Is this the 'beginning of the end'?" Some are Christians who have knowledge of Biblical prophecy. Others are those who wonder if such prophecies have any credibility. Impending death, whether it's our own or that of the world itself, causes us to consider whether this might mean the end as prophesied.

For us personally, the "beginning of the end" starts at birth. Our physical lives are nearer to the end with each breath. And Jesus speaks about the world's end: "Heaven and earth will pass away, but my words will not pass away. But concerning that day or hour no one knows, not even the angels in heaven, nor the Son, but the Father only." (Matthew 24:35-36) If all is ending, where is hope?

People who trust in Christ for His death, burial and resurrection on their behalf know death is not the end, because they have eternal life. We can also look forward to this— "...a new heaven and a new earth, for the first heaven and the first earth had passed away. . . Death shall be no more, neither shall there be mourning, nor crying, nor pain anymore, for the former things have passed away." (Revelation 21:1a, 4b)

Yes, what we know of this world, the beginning of the end is in motion, but it's not the end for those who trust the LORD. "Whoever hears my word and believes Him who sent me has eternal life. He does not come into judgment but has passed from death to life." (John 5:24)

How can we live this life on earth with the everlasting hope God promises through Christ? If you are unsure about whether you have such hope, visit this website: www.peacewithGod.net

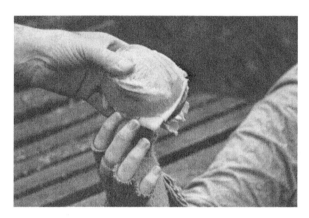

**Do not neglect to do good
and to share what you have,
for such sacrifices are
pleasing to God.**

- Hebrews 13:16

"Sharing Cookies"

And do not neglect to do good and to share what you have. . . .
~Hebrews 13:16a

Years ago, the mother of a college dormmate of mine sent packages of special cookies to her, instructing her to share them. They were delicious treasures and, occasionally, she would share them if we begged her. Most of the time she hid them, saving them for herself.

When I heard a sermon exhorting us to share Christ by proclaiming the gospel, I remembered those cookies. I considered how our friend was reluctant to share and how much we wanted them. I saw a connection to the gift we have by God's grace. We are not to keep what we possess in Christ hidden away for ourselves, rather we are to make known the heavenly riches with which we are blessed. God, like the "cookie maker," commands us to share the message of salvation with lost beggars, unlike the "cookie hoarder," who hid the treasures for herself.

Paul said it this way: "'Everyone who calls on the name of the LORD will be saved.' But how can they call on him to save them unless they believe in him? And how can they believe in him if they have never heard about him? And how can they hear about him unless someone tells them?" (Romans 10:13-14 NLT)

Our world is full of people hungering for truth, for grace, for nourishment to feed their souls. We need to reach out to them and share the glorious treasure we have. ". . . if someone asks about your hope as a believer, always be ready to explain it." (1 Peter 3:15b NLT) Sharing cookies is good for temporary gratification, but sharing the gospel offers eternal fulfillment.

If you know Jesus as your Savior, have you shared that "good news"? If you don't know Him, ask someone who does to share with you.

GREATER
L O V E
HAS NO MAN
Than This –
THAT
SOMEONE
lay down
HIS LIFE
FOR HIS
FRIENDS

"Micromartyrdom"

Greater love has no one than this: that someone lay down his life for his friends.
~ John 15:13

We've read about them—martyrs who died rather than deny Christ. As faithful followers, we like to believe, if the time or opportunity came, we would be "all in" too. Realistically, it's doubtful we will be put to that great test. But, to follow Christ's example, we must consider what He says: "Whoever wants to be my disciple must deny themselves and take up their cross daily and follow me." (Luke 9:23b NIV)

Could laying down our lives not mean a "once-for-all" event? Could sacrificing ourselves be an ongoing process, a kind of "micromartyrdom"—small, everyday surrenders of putting others' interests before ours? Could losing our lives in bits and pieces show the sacrificial love of Christ?

How is dying daily shown? By making time—to listen to others; to send an encouraging note or call a friend; to get up earlier to have devotions and pray for those we promised to pray for; to visit a shut-in; to serve at church or wherever needed.

We deny self by—allowing someone else to have—the remote, the last piece of our favorite pie, the window seat, the closest parking space, the pew where we usually sit, the last word.

Dying daily to self may mean—not responding to an offense in a like manner, whether in speech or action; forgiving slights and never recalling them to the slighter; withholding our opinions when unsolicited or unnecessary; not judging people on appearances; respecting the intrinsic value of each person God created. "Micromartyrdom" means laying down our lives daily in small considerations of Christlike love.

How do you show love by considering others before yourself? What can you do today to deny yourself for someone else?

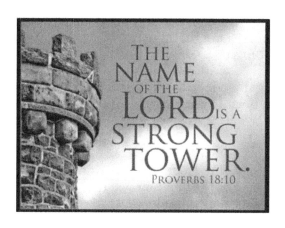

The Name of the Lord is a Strong Tower. Proverbs 18:10

"Where to Run for Help"

The name of the LORD is a strong tower; the righteous man runs into it and is safe.
~ Proverbs 18:10

Whenever fear or worry strikes, our minds race with questions. We tend to search for thoughts that give us a sense of safety and security. Recalling the words of hymns is one place to go. "Leaning on the Everlasting Arms" is one that gives safe thoughts, particularly to questions in the third verse, "What have I to dread, what have I to fear?" The answer? Nothing, if I'm leaning on God's arms.

Another song for anxious times is "Take it to the LORD in Prayer," especially the verse that asks, "Are we weak and heavy-laden, cumbered with a load of care?" and one that begs, "Is there trouble anywhere?" The answer—prayer. Indeed, the best place to run when circumstances overwhelm us is to the LORD himself and His Word. Isaiah tells us, "Fear not, for I am with you; do not be dismayed, for I am your God; I will strengthen you, I will help you, I will uphold you with my righteous right hand." (Isaiah 41:10 NIV)

Jesus exhorts us: "Therefore, do not be anxious, saying, 'What shall we eat?' or 'What shall we drink?' or 'What shall we wear?'. . . But seek first the kingdom of God and His righteousness, and all these things will be added to you." (Matthew 6:31a-34)

God's Word provides eternal, spiritual food: "Man shall not live by bread alone, but by every word that comes from the mouth of God." (Matthew 4:4 NASB) Let's run to the LORD in prayer and find sustenance for any situation in His faithful promises.

How can we make prayer a "first resort" and God our first resource when we need help?

My sheep hear my voice, and I know them, and they follow me. ~ JOHN 10:27

"My Special GPS"

My sheep hear my voice and I know them, and they follow me.
~John 10:27

Ever wonder how we made it anywhere without a GPS (Global Positioning System)? Don't get me wrong; I'm grateful for technology that helps directionally-challenged people like me. And, as I grow older and lose short-term memory brain cells, I'm hoping for a new advanced system to tell me why I went to the kitchen and what I went there to get.

Regardless of all the devices humans have created for directions or supplemental guidance, as a Christian believer, I have a GPS of far greater importance than any man-made invention—God's Preordained Shepherd. This GPS, provided by the one and only Almighty, Ever-present, All-knowing God, ensures that I am never lost or out of His reach, nor is He out of mine.

The psalmist writes: "Where can I go from your Spirit? Where can I flee from your presence? If I go up to the heavens, you are there; if I make my bed in the depths, you are there. If I rise on the wings of the dawn, if I settle on the far side of the sea, even there your hand will guide me, your right hand will hold me fast." (Psalm 139:7-9 NIV)

While the voice on a man-made global device tells me where to turn or which route is best while traveling, if I listen to the voice of Jesus, my Shepherd, I will end up where I belong—following Him as He guides me securely on the right path every day, which eventually will lead me safely home with Him.

How can we learn that we are in the presence of God and He is willing to guide us?

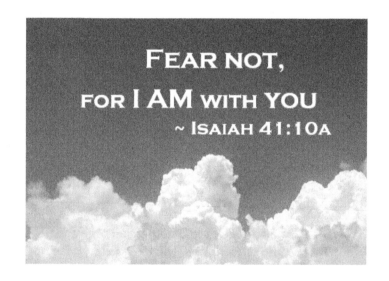

FEAR NOT,
FOR I AM WITH YOU
~ ISAIAH 41:10A

"No Separation Anxiety"

I will never leave you nor forsake you.
~Hebrews 13:5b

Ordinarily, we think young children are those most likely to have separation anxiety when parents leave them with a sitter or at school for the first time. But, as a mother, I was the one who suffered this malady at special times in our children's lives—when we dropped them off at college and when they walked down the wedding aisle. How hard those partings were, although I knew it wasn't a total farewell.

The most grievous separation anxiety of all is when death comes to those we love, and we are parted from them. The short-term separations we have in our lives cannot compare with that of death. Unless we die in a common event with loved ones, we will all feel the deep anguish of separation in every relationship. But, for Christians, there is one relationship we have that is the exception.

The single relationship in which believers will never experience separation is the one we have with Christ. We who've trusted in His saving grace have the assurance of His presence with us here, now, and forever. And another blessing is knowing that, although we may be separated from family and friends by death, we will be reunited someday with those who know Christ too. What comforting peace!

Simply put—no Jesus, know separation anxiety; know Jesus, no separation anxiety. Know Jesus, know peace. Nothing can separate us as written here: "For I am sure that neither death nor life, neither angels nor rulers, nor things present nor things to come, nor powers, nor height nor depth, nor anything else in creation, will be able to separate us from the love of God in Christ Jesus our Lord." (Romans 8:38-39)

How does knowing God will never leave you help you? How can you thank Him for His constant presence?

FORGET YOUR COMFORTABLE LIFE
...*whoever wants to be my disciple*

must DENY *themselves*
and
take up their CROSS
and
FOLLOW ME   ~ Mark 8:34 NIV

"WWJD or WWWD?"

Then he called the crowd to him along with his disciples and said:
'Whoever wants to be my disciple must deny themselves and take up
their cross and follow me.'
~ Mark 8:34 NIV

In the 1990's a popular acronym was "WWJD." Believers were to ask the question it represented—"What would Jesus do?"—whenever they came to a crisis of faith along their spiritual journey. Of course, this left the answer open to speculation on what believers "thought" Jesus would do. A better question to ask might be one represented by the acronym— "WDJD"—"What DID Jesus do?"

He demonstrated the love of the Father by coming to the world in the flesh and, by dying on a cross, made atonement for all our sins. He arose in victory over death, so we who accept His gift of grace might live forever, clothed in His righteousness. He calls us to follow His example. He said, "This is my commandment, that you love one another as I have loved you." (John 15:12) And He gave this directive: "Whoever wants to be my disciple must deny themselves and take up their cross and follow me." (Mark 8:34b NIV)

That should lead us to consider another acronym, "WWWD." The question here is, "What WILL we do?" Each day we have choices to make in how we will respond to relationships with difficult people or troubling circumstances. Will we choose to love, to forgive, to pray for our enemies, to be grateful for what we have rather than having everything we want, to be faithful in obedience to God regardless of how the world treats us? Will we do what Jesus did? It's up to us to choose what we will do that expresses what Jesus did.

Will the choices you make show the love of Christ to others and that you are willing to do as He did?

IN HIS
GREAT MERCY,
HE HAS GIVEN US
NEW BIRTH
→ INTO A ←
Living Hope
THROUGH THE
RESURRECTION OF
Jesus Christ
FROM THE DEAD
1 PETER 1:3

"Our Living Hope"

Blessed be the God and Father of our Lord Jesus Christ! According to his great mercy he has caused us to be born into a living hope through the resurrection of Jesus Christ from the dead.
~ 1 Peter 1:3

I am in an online support group for people who have a family member with a terminal disease. Some of the posts I read are filled with feelings ranging from anger to grief to despair. I find myself identifying with them, crying out to God at the thought of losing someone so dear.

As I read the posts of the online group, I think about how another support group may have experienced those same feelings on the day we call "Good Friday." What seemed to be the end of all hope for this group occurred at a place called Calvary, when they witnessed the death of Jesus on a cross between two thieves.

Then, I read other posts from my support group—expressions filled with gratitude, faith, and hope. And I think of another day long ago when Jesus' support group witnessed that first Easter. Christ rose victorious over death, fulfilling the promise that through Him, they have eternal life and so can everyone! I take heart in this glorious promise.

I ponder the fact that all of us are on the same journey toward leaving this life; death is the reality. But, for those who follow Christ, it is not the end— it's not Friday anymore—it's the Easter of our lives, our Resurrection Day. As we wait, we hang between two thieves, regrets of the past and fears of tomorrow. We have no control over either. Today—this moment—we can choose to be thankful for what we have—the constant love and presence of God, *our living hope*, to help, guide and strengthen us in our journey.

Is your hope in Christ, a living, vital assurance of your eternal destiny? Are you in His secure support group? If you are unsure, visit this website: www.peacewithGod.net

Count it all joy, my brothers, when you meet trials of various kinds, for you know the testing of your faith produces steadfastness ~

James 1:2~3

"Blessings in Disguise"

Count it all joy. . . when you meet trials of various kinds. . . .
~James 1:2

When considering our blessings we find it easy to count good health, financial security, pleasures, and even people we love. But, should we add such things as pain, failures, and stress?

Without pain, we'd have no twinges or sensations signaling something is wrong and needs attention. Our nerves send danger messages to the brain. Without such alarms, we could become incapacitated or die.

Our response to failures makes the difference in how we count them. Someone told Thomas Edison he was wasting time trying to create the light bulb, since he had failed so many times. He said they were just unsuccessful ways to find a workable one. Failures can lead to successes.

Being thankful for stress seems counterintuitive, but a study by The University of Buffalo showed benefits. Of 2400 people surveyed for four years, those who reported more adversity and difficulties had better mental health than those who had less. (Corbett, 2012) [2]

Consider how stress in nature yields positive results:

- Without struggling to shed its cocoon, the caterpillar would not become a butterfly.
- Without pressure and heat, a piece of coal would not become a diamond.
- Without an irritating grain of sand, an oyster would not produce a pearl.

Pain, failures, and stress are never part of life's pleasurable experiences, but they have purpose. We should: ". . .give thanks in all circumstances; for this is the will of God in Christ Jesus for you." (1 Thessalonians 5:18)

Have you ever experienced a blessing in disguise? How has that increased your faith?

---

2 Corbett, Holly C. (2012, April 9) *7 Weird Perks of Being Stressed.*
https://www.prevention.com/life/a20438709/acute-stress-may-be-good-for-your-health/

Though our outer self is wasting away. . .

. . .our inner self is being renewed day by day ~

2 Cor. 4-16

"Temple Ruins and Eternal Value"

Though our outer self is wasting away, our inner self is being renewed day by day.
~ 2 Corinthians 4:16b

Recently, a picture of ancient temple ruins appeared on my laptop monitor. I pondered what must have been a glorious structure in its time. Later, as I passed by a full-length mirror, I noted my body image boasting some obvious parallels to the ancient icon. My exterior showed signs of aging too—wrinkles, sagging skin, thinning hair. Then, I recalled an encouraging scripture about something eternal happening inside: "So, we do not lose heart. Though our outer self is wasting away, our inner self is being renewed day by day." (2 Corinthians 4:16)

As a Christian, my body is a temple. (1 Corinthians 6:19) While it will someday return to dust, what's inside—the Holy Spirit, united with my spirit through Christ, is indestructible, forever sealed as my guarantee of eternal life. Unlike the ancient temple, whatever was worshipped in it, real or mythical, is worthless compared to what my body houses.

We live in a culture that idolizes bodies, seeking endless means to keep them from aging, while we ignore our spirits. No amount of creams, tonics or plastic surgeries will prevent physical decay. Even Christians fall into the trap, trying to keep their temple exteriors from ruin. We need faith lifts, not face lifts. We need daily exercise—reading the Bible and doing deep knee bends in prayer to strengthen spiritual muscles. Certainly, we should maintain good health, but we need to remember what is of eternal importance: "For while bodily training is of some value, godliness is of value in every way, as it holds promise for both the present life and also for the life to come." (1 Timothy 4:8)

Do you perceive your spirit being renewed as you get older? What can you do to keep it in shape?

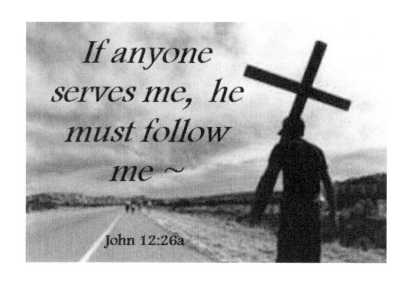

If anyone serves me, he must follow me ~

John 12:26a

"Whose 'Role Model' are You?"

If anyone serves me, he must follow me. . .
~ John 12:26a

A famous American athlete responded to the contention that he is a role model by claiming, "I am not a role model." He didn't want to be one, but nonetheless he is. In fact, everyone is a role model to someone. The parent is one to his child, the teacher to the student, the employer to the employee, the pastor to the congregant, the government leader to the citizen, and the athlete to the sports fan. It's not whether we believe we are role models or not; it's what kind we are or want to be.

The greatest role model of all time to all people is Jesus. More than anyone, He understood the importance of who He was and what He meant to the world. He didn't shrink from being the ultimate role model; He gave His life to save ours. His directive was clear, and He was explicit about what it means for those who choose to follow Him. He said, "I am the light of the world. Whoever follows me will never walk in darkness but will have the light of life." (John 8:12b) What an encouragement! At the same time, Jesus is forthcoming about the cost of following Him. "Whoever wants to be my disciple must deny themselves and take up their cross and follow me." (Mark 8:34 NIV)

The apostle Paul emulated Christ in his life and declared the principle of role modeling to believers, "Follow my example as I follow the example of Christ." (1 Corinthians 11:1 NIV) It's true. If we follow Jesus, we will model the best to anyone looking to us as a role model.

Who is your role model of faith? How can you follow Christ's example to be a role model to others?

"Letting Things Go"

Autumn - the trees are about to show us how lovely it is to let things go.
~ Anonymous

Some people are blessed to live in parts of the U.S where deciduous trees mark the fall season with painted landscapes. The glorious colors of sugar maple and red oak create a palette of autumn hues—gold, rust, and scarlet dotting hillsides like an artist's canvas. They render a splendid fall show before they let go.

As we watch such trees shed their leaves, we can consider how true it is of the seasons of our lives when we "let things go." Some things, like the leaves on the trees, are a part of the life cycle about which we have no choice but to let go. Aging for us means other kinds of losses— hair, vision, hearing, skin tone and memory—not so "lovely" to let go but a part of life.

However, unlike trees, and as believers in Christ, we can find it is lovelier to let go of things that hamper us from moving on to God's plan and purpose for our spiritual maturity. We can choose to do as Paul did, ". . . forgetting what lies behind and straining forward to what lies ahead, I press on toward the goal for the prize of the upward call of God in Christ Jesus." (Philippians 3:13b-14)

With God's help, we can "put off" such things as grudges, guilt, worry, hurts, fear and failures, those things that hinder our lives from being fruitful. The loveliness of letting them go will produce fruit of the Spirit— love, joy, peace, forbearance, kindness, goodness, faithfulness, gentleness, and self-control.

What "keepsakes" do you have that are lovely? What ones should you be letting go?

John 11:25-26

Jesus said to her,
"I am the resurrection and the life.
He who believes in Me,
though he may die, he shall live.

And whoever lives
and believes in Me shall never die.
Do you believe this?"

"Good News – A Cure for Cancer"

Jesus said. . . 'I am the resurrection and the life. Whoever believes in me, though he die, yet shall he live.'
~John 11:25

The statistics show that nearly everyone reading this has either had cancer or knows a friend or family member who has this dreaded disease. Its scourge brings loss of health and loss of life to millions. While new treatments appear in the news almost daily providing hope, the best news would be for a cure to end all forms of it.

The good news is—a cure for one form of cancer does exist, available to all who suffer from it and, according to the Bible, everyone ever born suffers from it. It's the spiritual cancer of sin. It came into the world when the first man and woman chose to disobey God and yield to temptation. The sin "cancer" meant physical and spiritual death for all mankind. But God, in His sovereign mercy and grace, provided a cure. Through the physical death and resurrection of Jesus Christ, He offers eternal life for those who believe! "He himself bore our sins in his body on the tree, that we might die to sin and live to righteousness. By his wounds you have been healed." (1 Peter 2:24)

While physical cancer still abounds, we search and pray for a cure, but we who have victory over the cancer of sin and death through Christ offer good news. Our physical bodies may succumb to cancer, but they will be resurrected. "If the Spirit of him who raised Jesus from the dead dwells in you, he who raised Christ Jesus from the dead will also give life to your mortal bodies through his Spirit who dwells in you." (Romans 8:11)

Do you know the One who can heal the spiritual cancer of sin? Have you asked Him to heal you and give you eternal life? If not, go to this website: www.peacewithGod.net

For you were called to
freedom, brothers.
Only do not use your
freedom as an
opportunity for the
flesh, but through
LOVE
serve one another.
~ Galatians 5:13

"Liberty, not License"

For you were called to freedom, brothers. Only do not use your freedom
as an opportunity for the flesh, but through love, serve one another.
~Galatians 5:13

One of Jesus' promises to His followers was that they would know the truth and it would set them free. (John 8:31-32) The truth is Christ Himself and what He did was to free us from slavery to sin. He paid the penalty for our sins by dying on the cross, so we would not be held accountable.

Does this mean we are free to live as we please? Some early believers considered such grace to be a license to do whatever they wanted. Paul's letter to the Romans addressed this when he asked, "Are we to sin because we are not under law, but under grace? By no means!" (Romans 6:15)

Notice the letters of the word "liberty" are found within the word "responsibility." The definition of "liberty" as "the power of choice" demonstrates how such freedom is not unrestricted. Freedom is not license, which means "to use freedom with irresponsibility." Notice the letters of the word "license" also appear in the word "licentiousness," from the same Latin root. To consider the grace of Christ as a license to sin sullies the cross, rendering it useless for salvation unto righteousness.

Jesus freed us from the penalty of sin, but we are not free from sin's presence in this current world. As followers of Christ, however, we have the power of the Holy Spirit to help us use our liberty with responsibility. We are to ". . . live as people who are free, not using. . .freedom as a cover-up for evil, but 'living as servants' of God." (1 Peter 2:16)

How can we make responsible choices for the liberty Christ has given us?

I am the *VINE*;

you are the branches.

Whoever abides in me

and I in him, he it is that

bears much fruit,

for apart from

 ME, you can do

nothing. ~John 15:5

"The Pruning Principle"

*I am the vine; you are the branches. Whoever abides in me and I in him,
he it is that bears much fruit. . .*
~John 15:5

My father, an avid gardener, understood the principle of pruning. Each spring he wielded his shears on overgrown shrubs and trees. He knew pruning allowed plants' support systems to send vital energy and nutrients to smaller areas, encouraging more vigorous growth. The plants flourished in appearance, and their flower and fruit production increased.

My mother applied the same spring-cleaning principle to every drawer and closet inside our house. We "pruned" whatever we weren't using or wearing. Clothes, toys, books, and knick-knacks soon made their way to other families or charities. Not only did our house improve in appearance, but with less stuff to manage, we experienced a sense of order and peace.

Jesus understood the pruning principle too, as it applies to our spiritual lives. He said, "I am the true vine, and my Father is the vinedresser. Every branch in me that does not bear fruit he takes away, and every branch that does bear fruit he prunes, that it may bear more fruit." (John 15:1-2) We must submit to God's pruning to bear fruit. He will help us rid our lives of excess, whether material things, negative attitudes, or destructive habits. We will become less stressed, less depressed, healthier, and more energetic in body and spirit. And who would not want to produce the fruit of the Spirit—love, joy, peace, patience, kindness, goodness, gentleness, faithfulness, and self-control?

What do you need to "prune" from your "inner" garden—thoughts, speech, or actions, allowing the Spirit to bear His fruit?

GREAT

are the works

of the

LORD ~

Psalm 111:2

"God-Incidents"

Great are the works of the Lord, studied by all who delight in them. He has caused his wondrous works to be remembered; the Lord is gracious and merciful.
~Psalm 111:2, 4

Stories appear in books and online about how uncanny incidents occur to people. Some dismiss such happenings as coincidences, but as a Christian, I believe they are God-Incidents, happenings He has planned to occur well in advance of their happening. I know, because He planned this one:

When my dearest friend, Marlene, was dying from a brain tumor, I wrote her name in my Bible by a psalm that illustrated her strong faith. "Nevertheless, I am continually with you; you hold my right hand. You guide me with your counsel, and afterward you will receive me to glory. Whom have I in heaven but you? And there is nothing on earth that I desire besides you. My flesh and my heart may fail, but God is the strength of my heart and my portion forever." (Psalm 73:23-26)

Several months later, as she approached the doorway to heaven, I spoke with her husband, who knew that she and I read the same daily devotional. He shared how she had been highlighting ones of future dates. He asked me to read the one for the upcoming Saturday. It was a devotional based on Psalm 73:23-26! I choked as I told him how I had written her name by the same passage months before. A God-Incident!

On that very highlighted Saturday, Marlene entered heaven's gates, but God was not finished. When her husband called their pastor to plan her service, the pastor said he had chosen some special verses, subject to the husband's approval, and they were the same verses in Psalm 73! How gracious of God "to cause his wondrous works to be remembered." When the LORD received Marlene to glory, He comforted us by His word, and assured us of His plan and purpose for "all who delight in him."

What God-incidents have you experienced? How can you share those as evidence of His faithfulness in your life?

Standing on the promises of God ~

"Standing on the Promises of God"

For all the promises of God find their "Yes" in him [Christ]. That is why it
is through him that we utter "Amen" to God for his glory
~ 2 Corinthians 1:20

An old-time hymn, "Standing on the Promises of God," illustrates how God's Word gives assurances to guide and guard every believer's life. Depending on the source and version, from three to over seven thousand promises exist in the Bible. The hymn-writer knew God's Word is a strong foundation for faith, but how can we stand on the promises if we don't know them?

The writer of Psalm 119 reveals how God's word undergirded his life with hope, truth, and protection. In the 176 verses of the psalm, all but five include references to various synonyms for the scriptures, illustrating the importance and power of knowing them. The writer declares his own promise to the LORD and acknowledges God's promise, "The LORD is my portion; I promise to keep your words. I entreat your favor with all my heart; be gracious to me according to your promise." (Psalm 119:57-58)

God's promises are powerful. We can find them in every book of the Bible and, if we "dig" into it and "mine" them like gold, we will enjoy wealth beyond measure, kept as our treasure in heaven. Here are three mighty promises: God assures us He will never leave us or forsake us (Hebrews 5:13); He has given us eternal life through Christ's death and resurrection (John 3:16); and nothing can separate us from His love. (Romans 8:38-39)

No matter how many of the thousands of promises we choose to discover and claim, we will form a foundation on which we can sing with knowledge: "Standing, standing, I'm standing on the promises of God!"

What promises of God do you "stand" on? How can making a list of those or memorizing them help you "stand" on them and increase your faith?

We know for those who love God
all things work together for good,
for those who are called according to
his purpose.
    For those he foreknew he also
predestined to be conformed to the
    image of his son.

                        ~ Romans 8:28-29a

"Storage Boxes"

And we know that for those who love God all things work together for good, for those who are called according to his purpose. For those whom he foreknew he also predestined to be conformed to the image of his Son.
~Romans 8:28-29a

Barbara Johnson, beloved Christian author, wrote over twenty-five books, including "Pack up your Gloomies in a Great Big Box, then Sit on the Lid and Laugh." Johnson experienced many troubles in her life, and she covered them with a strong faith, expressed through the lenses of humor.

We have storage boxes too, where we keep memories, including hurts and disappointments. Rather than "sitting on them and laughing," we tend to bring them out, grieving and reliving them. Hurts are not laughable but, as Christians, we can find perspective in them.

How can we learn to respond to troubles so we can grow spiritually? In the book of James, we are told: "Count it all joy. . .when you meet trials of various kinds, for you know that the testing of your faith produces steadfastness." (James 1:2-3) Jesus himself assures us of our peace in Him, despite troubles. "In the world you will have tribulation. But take heart; I have overcome the world." (John 16:33b)

When we consider our hurts, perhaps we can picture a box with the name "Jesus" on it. As Peter suggests, we can pack away our cares in it, by "casting all your anxieties on him, because he cares for you." (1 Peter 5:7)

Johnson created boxes called "Joy", where she put keepsakes—notes and cards from readers, special Bible verses and other treasures. She filled a whole room in her house with them, named "the Joy Room." They reminded her of how God was using their contents to conform her to the image of Christ. He is doing the same with us no matter what we might name our boxes of experiences.

What name would you give your "keepsake" box of experiences? How can God use our experiences to conform us to Christ's image?

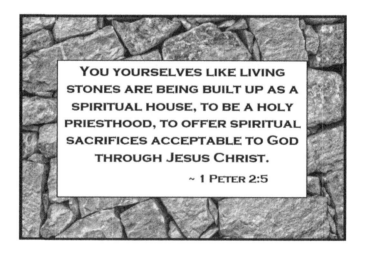

YOU YOURSELVES LIKE LIVING
STONES ARE BEING BUILT UP AS A
SPIRITUAL HOUSE, TO BE A HOLY
PRIESTHOOD, TO OFFER SPIRITUAL
SACRIFICES ACCEPTABLE TO GOD
THROUGH JESUS CHRIST.

~ 1 PETER 2:5

"Precious Commodities"

...you yourselves like living stones are being built up... to be a holy priesthood, to offer spiritual sacrifices acceptable to God through Jesus Christ.
~ 1 Peter 2:5

People hold certain commodities to be precious—gold, silver, copper, and diamonds. They become more valuable and useful after going through a refining process. Metals require high temperatures to remove impurities and dross; diamonds must be cut and polished to gain their highest quality.

God holds us believers as most precious too. We are called "living stones," who go through sanctification, the process of being made holy and set apart—like Christ. This begins the moment we believe in Christ for salvation. "For by a single offering, he has perfected for all time those who are being sanctified." (Hebrews 10:14)

Like raw precious metals and diamonds, the Holy Spirit refines us into "living stones." Paul encouraged the Philippians in the process to "... work out your own salvation with fear and trembling, for it is God who works in you, both to will and to work for his good pleasure." (Philippians 2:12b-13)

While refined precious minerals and gems are finished when they meet the highest standards, we will not reach perfection until Christ comes and we are in His presence. Paul's prayer for the Thessalonians can apply to us, "Now, may the God of peace himself sanctify you completely, and may your whole spirit and soul and body be kept blameless at the coming of our Lord Jesus Christ." (1 Thessalonians 5:23)

We may get discouraged while living in a sinful, fallen world, but our faithful God keeps "polishing" us. Paul wrote to believers in Philippi, "...he who began a good work in you will bring it to completion in the day of Jesus Christ." (Philippians 1:6) He will do the same in us.

Do you perceive how God is working in you to help you become more like Christ? How does this help you grow in faith?

All we like

Sheep

have

gone

astray — Isaiah 53:6

"All We Like Sheep. . ."

When he saw the crowds, he had compassion for them. . . they were harassed and helpless, like sheep without a shepherd.
~ Matthew 9:36

God compares people to sheep many times in the Bible, and we humans bear some "sheep" characteristics. Sheep are nearsighted and wander, much like we do when we lose focus on our Shepherd. Isaiah writes, "All we like sheep have gone astray; we have turned—every one—to his own way." (Isaiah 53:6a)

Sheep are not beasts of burden, nor are we designed to be, but we tend to carry grudges or worries God doesn't want us to bear. Scripture tells us to give these to God. "Cast all your anxiety on him because he cares for you." (1 Peter 5:7 NIV)

Unlike some animals, sheep are defenseless against predators. If they fall on their backs, they cannot right themselves and will die without help. We are helpless to save ourselves, but God offers us eternal life. ". . . that while we were still sinners, Christ died for us."(Romans 5:8)

Sheep follow the voice of whoever is leading them. If we follow Jesus, He will lead us in paths of righteousness. He says, "My sheep hear my voice, and I know them, and they follow me." (John 10:27) Sheep are valuable. They provide milk, meat, parchment, and fleece. God values us, adopting us through Christ to provide service. "For we are his workmanship, created in Christ Jesus for good works. . . (Ephesians 2:10a) We, like sheep, need a caretaker, the Good Shepherd, the Chief Shepherd—Jesus.

What features do you have as a sheep in God's "flock"? How can you thank the Shepherd for His care?

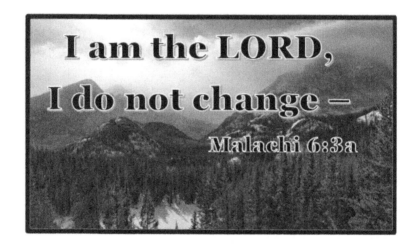

I am the LORD,
I do not change –
Malachi 6:3a

"Changes and Choices"

For I the LORD do not change
~ Malachi 3:6a

Many people believe the two things in life we cannot avoid are death and taxes. For us Christians who believe in the rapture of Christ, death could be avoided should Christ come before we die. (1 Thessalonians 4:16-17) And we can avoid paying taxes—with consequences.

Life does include two unavoidable things—changes and choices. As you read this, your very body is changing, discarding and replacing cells by the millions. The atmosphere and weather are in constant flux. Only one thing in the universe never changes—the person of God. His immutability is declared in Malachi 3:6a and is reiterated in the book of Hebrews: "Jesus Christ is the same yesterday and today and forever." (Hebrews 13:8)

What about choices? Humans make as many as 35,000 a day, either subconsciously or consciously. You are choosing to read this now over something else you could be doing. Some choices have short term results; others have long term ones. If we watch a late TV show, we may be groggy the following day. If we choose an unhealthy lifestyle, we may develop a harmful, even fatal, disease.

There is one single choice, however, that affects our eternity. Where we spend eternity depends on the choice we make about Jesus Christ. His death, burial and resurrection redeemed us to live forever. As sinners all, we can choose to accept or reject Him as our Savior. "For God so loved the world, that he gave his only Son, that whoever believes in him should not perish but have eternal life. Whoever believes in him is not condemned, but whoever does not believe is condemned already, because he has not believed in the name of the only Son of God." (John 3:16,18)

Changes and choices are unavoidable, and one choice is paramount.

What changes have you learned to accept over which you have no control? Have you made the choice to accept Christ as your Savior?

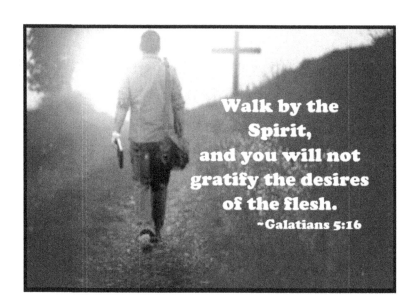

Walk by the Spirit, and you will not gratify the desires of the flesh.
~Galatians 5:16

"Unhealthy Exercises"

Rather train yourself for godliness; for while bodily training is of some value, godliness is of value in every way.
~ 1 Timothy 4:7b-8a

Physical exercise is necessary for keeping our bodies in condition and healthy, but Christians should beware of harmful spiritual exercises:

<u>Jumping to Conclusions</u>—When we judge by appearances, we do not see a person's character the way God does. "For the Lord sees not as man sees; man looks on the outward appearance, but the Lord looks on the heart." (1 Samuel 16:7b) And we are warned about making such judgments by Jesus: "Judge not, that you be not judged. For with the judgment you pronounce you will be judged." (Matthew 7:1-2a)

<u>Hopping Mad</u>—God knows we can get angry, but he wants us to "temper" our tempers. James writes, ". . . let every person be quick to hear, slow to speak, slow to anger; for the anger of man does not produce the righteousness of God." (James 1:19b-20) Also, "Whoever is slow to anger has great understanding, but he who has a hasty temper exalts folly." (Proverbs 14:29)

<u>Grudge-bearing</u>—Carrying the weight of unforgiveness builds bitterness, especially in the heart muscle. Christ forgave our sins by bearing them on the cross, the ultimate example for us to follow. "Be kind to one another, tenderhearted, forgiving one another, as God in Christ forgave you." (Ephesians 4:32) By refusing to forgive, we presume upon God's grace: "For if you forgive others their trespasses, your heavenly Father will also forgive you." (Matthew 6:14)

Christians do well to replace ungodly "exercises" with ones of eternal value. The simplest one is to ". . .walk by the Spirit, and you will not gratify the desires of the flesh." (Galatians 5:16b)

Are you doing any of these spiritually unhealthy exercises? How can you choose ones to make you more spiritually "fit?"

If anyone is in Christ
he is a new creation. . .
the new has come. . .
2 Corinthians 5:17

"Glorious Makeover"

So, we do not lose heart. Though our outer self is wasting away, our inner self is being renewed day by day. For this light momentary affliction is preparing for us an eternal weight of glory beyond all comparison, as we look not to the things that are seen but to the things that are unseen. For the things that are seen are transient, but the things that are unseen are eternal.
~ 2 Corinthians 4:16-18

Some people read the Bible for inspiration; others read it for information. While both are worthy goals, the object of God's Word is for the reader's transformation. The gospel of John says, "But these [words] are written so that you may believe that Jesus is the Christ, the Son of God, and that by believing you may have life in his name." (John 20:31)

Once a person believes in Christ for salvation, the "makeover" begins. ". . . if anyone is in Christ, he is a new creation. The old has passed away; behold, the new has come." (2 Corinthians 5:17) Most of us might wish the transformation to be one of a new, younger body with smooth skin, thick hair, firm-toned muscles, and renewed brain cells. But His makeover is an "inside job;" the Holy Spirit is working within us to transform our character into the image of Christ.

Paul's encouragement to believers who are aging is found in 2 Corinthians 4:16-18. We are being made new creatures on the inside day by day. "And we all. . . are being transformed into the same image from one degree of glory to another. For this comes from the Lord who is the Spirit." (2 Corinthians 3:18) It's a complete, glorious makeover!

Have you ever tried products or regimens to stop or slow aging? Do you see your inner self being transformed or have you never become that new creation in Christ? If not, visit: www.peacewithGod.net

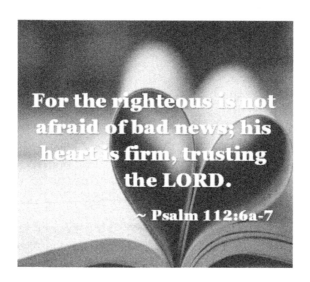

For the righteous is not afraid of bad news; his heart is firm, trusting the LORD.

~ Psalm 112:6a-7

"Good News, Bad News"

For the righteous. . . is not afraid of bad news; his heart is firm, trusting in the LORD.
~ Psalm 112:6a-7

News—it comes by newspaper, mail, TV, texts, and social media. We have a hunger for the latest. A friend of mine, who lived before the tech age, confessed how she hurried each morning to read the newspaper, only to be disappointed, because there was no "new" news and most of it was bad. Thousands of years ago, the writer of Ecclesiastes made the same observation: ". . .there is nothing new under the sun." (1:9b)

Yes, new inventions and technologies have changed our way of life, but the basic nature of this fallen world is the same. Natural disasters still occur, death comes to all creatures, and people continue to murder, steal, and commit all kinds of sin. Most "news" is devoted to these same events; only the names of people or places change as they recur.

My friend realized she was looking in the wrong place for encouraging "news." She started beginning each day with a timeless source—the Bible. Could this ancient book provide anything new? Indeed. "For the word of God is *living and active*, sharper than any two-edged sword. . ." (Hebrews 4:12a) And this verse underscores its power: "All Scripture is breathed out by God and profitable for teaching, for reproof, for correction, and for training in righteousness." (2 Timothy 3:16)

The writer of Ecclesiastes came to a similar conclusion—that revering God and obeying His Word gives meaning to life in this world: "The end of the matter; all has been heard. Fear God and keep his commandments, for this is the whole duty of man." (Ecclesiastes 12:13) The world is full of bad news, but trusting God and His promises is good news every day.

What is your "news" source each day for encouragement? Do you have a Bible reading or Bible study plan?

"But one thing is necessary. Mary has chosen the good **portion,** which will not be taken away from her."

Luke 10:42

"Hostess Hysteria"

...Jesus...came to a village where a woman named Martha opened her home to him. She had a sister called Mary, who sat at the Lord's feet listening to what he said. But Martha was distracted by all the preparations that had to be made. She came to him and asked, 'Lord, don't you care that my sister has left me to do the work by myself? Tell her to help me!'
~Luke 10:38-40

When reading this account of Mary and Martha, I readily identify with Martha. Many times, when I entertain people, I am fraught with trying to make everything a "Martha," even an ala Martha Stewart experience. While others enjoy time together, I am distracted, obsessed with making an "ideal hostess" production. I miss extending true hospitality—a warm, friendly welcoming for personal connection, instead of an all-consuming staged setting of perfection.

Yes, I want my offerings to guests to be orderly and fulfilling, but as Jesus told Martha, "few things are needed." Spending time with guests should take priority over excessive details. Jesus says that Mary chose the "better thing," giving attention to Him. He did not discount Martha's work, but it overshadowed her enjoying His presence.

While I sympathize with Martha, I realize my hysteria is a vain desire to gain favor from others and God. It doesn't matter if the table setting is askew, if I have flour on my blouse, or I let the bread overbake. I need to replace "hostess hysteria" with "hostess hospitality," welcoming guests in my home as if I were welcoming Jesus to enjoy His presence. Seeing guests in that regard will be a blessing to them and me. I will be choosing the better thing.

Have you ever entertained and were so consumed with serving you missed spending time with guests? How can we balance serving with enjoying our company?

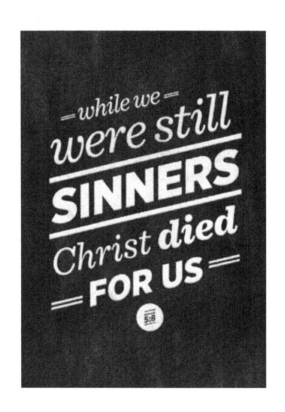

"Mercy or Justice"

...but God shows his love for us in that while we were still sinners, Christ died for us.
~Romans 5:8

Imagine yourself being careless while driving and finding you've gone over the speed limit. You notice a flashing light behind you and recognize a police car. As you pull over, do you start praying for mercy? When you get only a warning ticket, you sigh in relief. Would you have the same prayer for someone whom you saw zoom by you with excessive speed when you come upon them pulled over by the police? Would you pray mercy for the driver or hope the policeman issues a full speeding ticket?

We tend to want mercy for our failings but justice for the other person's. As Christians, Jesus taught us what he called the second commandment. Closely related to the first—loving God—we are to love other people. Paul expresses it this way, "For the whole law is fulfilled in one word: 'You shall love your neighbor as yourself.'" (Galatians 5:14) If we want mercy for ourselves, shouldn't we also want it for our neighbor?

Our God of grace and mercy shows Himself to be longsuffering by not giving us what we deserve. The ultimate act of love was sending Jesus to take our sin upon Himself as the perfect sacrificial atonement through His blood on the cross to reconcile us to holy God. By His resurrection He gave us eternal life. We, who deserve justice for our sins, receive amazing grace instead. Should we not want that for any other sinner?

Let's desire others to receive the same grace we have, "that supplications, prayers, intercessions, and thanksgivings be made for all people. . . pleasing in the sight of God our Savior, who desires all people to be saved and to come to the knowledge of the truth." (1 Timothy 2:1a, 3-4)

Do you struggle with showing the same mercy to others that you enjoy? How can we extend mercy and allow God to mete out justice?

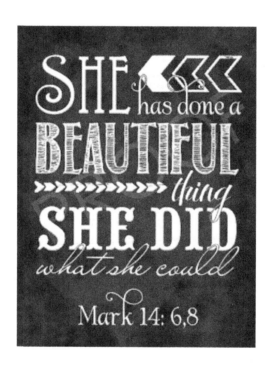

"My Offerings"

She did what she could.
~ Mark 14:8

There's something about some canvas artists that I envy. When they render a painting and declare it finished, it is. They make no touch-ups or add-ons. It's different for me. As a writer, I'm forever second-guessing my devotionals. I edit and re-edit, seeking to turn a better phrase or refine the message. I wonder if readers will think them worthy.

I read a story in Mark's gospel that gave me a new perspective about how an offering is perceived. Mark tells about the woman who anointed Jesus with expensive perfume from an alabaster jar. Her act caused others at the occasion to indignantly rebuke her. They said it would have been better to sell the oil and give the proceeds to the poor. Jesus said, "Why are you bothering her? She has done a beautiful thing to me. The poor you will always have with you...but you will not always have me. She did what she could." (Mark 14:6-8) He went on to say her anointing was for His coming burial and that she would be remembered for it.

Five words from the story struck me. "She did what she could." What she did was costly, not only in terms of the value of the perfume, but in performing her act of devotion in front of a critical audience, with one exception. Jesus saw it as a precious gift from her heart of love. Perhaps what we offer is more a matter of how the LORD views it rather than how others do. He knows our hearts and our motives. Paul tells us, "Whatever you do, work heartily, as for the Lord and not for men." (Colossians 3:23)

I want to "do what I can" to write words that glorify the LORD. If those who read them understand that, then He is blessed even more.

Are you doing what you can to serve the LORD, to please Him? How can you use your gifts to give Him glory?

11 For the sun rises with its scorching heat and withers the grass; its flower falls, and its beauty perishes. So also will the rich man fade away in the midst of his pursuits.

James 1

12 Blessed is the m[...] [un]der trial, [f]or when he has stood the test he wi[...] [...]hich G[...] has promised to those who love hi[m].

13 Let no one say when he is tempted, "I am being tempted by God." for God cannot be tempted with evil, and he himself tempts no one.

14 But each person is tempted when he is lured and enticed by his own desire.

15 Then desire when it has conceived gives birth to sin, and sin when it is fully grown brings forth death.

16 Do not be deceived, my beloved brothers.

17 Every good gift and every perfect gift is from above, coming down from the Father of lights with whom there is no variation or shadow due to change.

"Nibbles"

And lead us not into temptation, but deliver us from evil.
~ Matthew 6:13

In the '60's a snack food advertisement used the phrase, "Betcha Can't Eat Just One!" It was effective in proving how we can lose restraint. Small concessions lead to bigger problems. We tell ourselves that one little nibble won't hurt, but soon we've noshed our way into trouble. Didn't Adam and Eve do that with a bite of forbidden fruit? The devil was the first master of effective marketing to the base nature of humankind.

False teachers of the Christian faith follow the same pattern, luring people to consider ideas or behaviors that are not from God. Christians hear something that seems innocuous, so they nibble, chew and ingest it. Jesus warned His followers about the "leaven of the Pharisees," who touted salvation by works, not faith. Paul used the same metaphor: "Do you not know that a little leaven leavens the whole lump?" (1 Corinthians 5:6a)

When we taste a "morsel" marketed as God's truth, we could be nibbling our way into doubt and unbelief. Jesus Himself warned us: "Beware of false prophets, who come to you in sheep's clothing...you will know them by their fruits." (Matthew 7:15-16a) Also, James tells us to test spirits, "... do not believe every spirit but test the spirits to see whether they are from God, for many false prophets have gone out into the world."(1 John 1:4)

How do we test? By checking teachings against scripture. "All Scripture is breathed out by God and profitable for teaching, for reproof, for correction, and for training in righteousness." (2 Timothy 3:16) When tempted to nibble something being taught as if it's from God, we need to check it against His written word.

Do you search the scriptures to see if something you read or hear aligns with Biblical truth? How can Bible study help us to recognize false teaching?

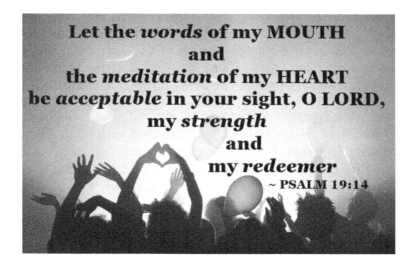

Let the *words* of my MOUTH
and
the *meditation* of my HEART
be *acceptable* in your sight, O LORD,
my *strength*
and
my *redeemer*
~ PSALM 19:14

"Words"

*Let the words of my mouth and the meditation of my heart be acceptable
in your sight, O LORD, my strength and my redeemer*
~ Psalm 19:14 NKJV

Words. We speak them; we hear them; we read them; we write them. Their significance is beyond measure; our world would not exist without them. Through His spoken word, God created the heavens, the earth, the sun, the moon, the stars and the sea, air, dry land, and their creatures. He said, "Let there be. . ." and all of these came into existence.

The only creatures God did not speak into existence were the first man and woman; He formed them in His own image, giving them the ability to communicate with words. Through the Holy Spirit, He inspired special men—prophets, kings, servants—to inscribe and record His Words into the Old Testament of the Bible.

God wasn't finished with words once the Old Testament was written. We find the epitome of God's Word in the New Testament gospel of John: "In the beginning was the Word and the Word was with God. He was in the beginning with God." (John 1:1-2) He sent Jesus, the Word, "logos" in Greek, meaning He is the total message God wanted to send to us. John used the Word, meaning Jesus, to communicate the Second Person of the Trinity, as the self-expression of God to the world. "And the Word became flesh and dwelt among us, and we have seen his glory, glory as of the only Son from the Father, full of grace and truth." (John 1:14)

Words. What a special gift God has given us in them and in the Word made flesh. How we use words reflects the Word God sent us in Christ. If our words are rendered with grace and truth, they will bring glory to the Father, Son and Holy Spirit.

How do you use words? Do you treat them with care, so they reflect the Word?

And
my God will
supply
every need
of yours
according
to his riches
in glory in
Christ
Jesus.

PHILIPPIANS 4:19 ESV

"Thanks, and Yes, Thanks!"

And my God will supply every need of yours according to his riches in glory in Christ Jesus.
~ Philippians 4:19

"Thanks, but no, thanks." That's a response we sometimes give when we don't appreciate a gift nor want it. We receive some things over which we have no choice. We have no choice about where we are born, the members of our biological family, or our physical appearance at birth. We may not perceive them as gifts or feel grateful for them, yet the bottom line of contentment in life is to have gratitude for whatever we have. True thanksgiving comes from a heart of contentment. It is in wanting what we have rather than in having what we lack or desire.

Paul says that he has "learned the secret of being content in *any* and *every* situation." (Philippians 4:12b) How? By the power of Christ in him that he shares in verse 13: "I can do all things through Him who strengthens me."

To encourage us, Paul states a wonderful promise in verse 19 in the same chapter, "And my God will supply every need of yours according to his riches in glory in Christ Jesus." Notice that he doesn't say God will meet all your wants. So, what do we need? As followers we need to be like Him, to choose in loving obedience to do God's will by accepting whatever circumstances come and thanking Him in the process, trusting Him to work out His will for us.

We may never *feel* gratitude for things we cannot change, but we can thank God in faithful assurance that He will use them for His good purposes and His glory—the fulfillment of His promise in Romans 8:28-29, that He is working everything to conform us to the image of Christ. Therefore, let us say, no matter what, "Thanks, and yes, thanks!"

How can we develop an attitude of gratitude to God *in* all things?

Let your
LIGHT
shine before
others

"This Little Light"

Again, Jesus spoke to them saying, "I am the light of the world. Whoever follows me will never walk in darkness but will have the light of life."
~ John 8:12

A sudden blackout occurred one evening during a storm, causing total darkness in our home and neighborhood. All the electronic devices we are blessed to enjoy—the iPad, TV, telephone, as well as our lights and appliances—succumbed to the power outage. We were bummed.

Then, I recalled Ben Franklin's advice: "Instead of cursing the darkness, light a candle." I managed to navigate through the dark to find that ancient alternative tucked away in a drawer. With one click of a lighter, the small, soft glow of the burning taper dispelled the blackness in the room.

The luminance of the candle fascinated me. As I watched it yield its wax to the flaming wick, I marveled at the power of one little light to penetrate the darkness. I thought of another Light that we recall and celebrate—the Light that came into this dark world over two thousand years ago bringing hope and love, fulfilling a promise made in heaven.

Could it be that if we would choose to shine our own light—no matter how small or limited—it would dispel the gloom in our little corner of the world? Could we follow that example of long ago—Jesus Christ, the Light of the world—to shine in a measure of our own? It's possible. In fact, as believers we are called to do just that, as Jesus directed in Matthew 5:16: "Let your light shine before others, so they may see your good works and give glory to your Father who is in heaven." Rather than cursing the darkness, we can be like one small candle, letting our little light shine.

How can you shine your light in a world that appears full of darkness and gloom? What one thing can you do today to light up the world around you?

For by **GRACE** *you have been saved through* **FAITH**.
And this is not your own doing; it is the **GIFT** *of GOD.*

EPHESIANS 2:8

"The Christmas Gift Exchange"

For by grace you have been saved through faith, and this is not your own doing, it is the gift of God.
~ Ephesians 2:8

The popular cultural tradition of giving gifts at Christmas is, in many cases, merely an exchange. We give gifts to others because they give gifts to us. The practice is a trade transaction rather than actual "gift-giving." Dictionary.com defines a gift as "something given voluntarily to someone without payment in return." When we give something to someone who cannot give us anything in return or who is not expected to do so—it's a gift.

On that first Christmas centuries ago, God gave us a gift and provided an exchange. God sent Jesus, His Son, to be born in human form to redeem us. His death on the cross as an atoning sacrifice was the unmerited gift. And it was an exchange—His shed blood is payment for all our sins, freeing us from condemnation. His resurrection—conquering death—is a gift to all who believe and receive Him, ensuring eternal life instead of eternal death. God did it all in one amazing grace transaction. He gave the gift and made the exchange. We did nothing to earn or deserve the gift, nor could we give anything back in exchange. "For the wages of sin is death, but the free gift of God is eternal life in Christ Jesus our Lord." (Romans 6:23) And, if that wasn't enough, He gives us His Spirit as an ongoing gift!

"Thanks be to God for his inexpressible gift!" (2 Corinthians 9:15)

Do you give gifts without any expectation from the recipients? Do you feel obligated to give a gift to someone who gives you one? How can we give with the same grace God gives us? If you have never received His gift, visit www.peacewithGod.net

The TRUE LIGHT which gives light to everyone was coming into the world

~ John 1:9

"Whose Birthday Is it Anyway?"

The true light, which gives light to everyone, was coming into the world.
He was in the world...
~John 1:9-10a

Colored paper, empty boxes and ribbon covered the living room floor, evidence that our family lived up to the cultural expectations of exchanging Christmas gifts. We were leaving on vacation the next day, so we needed to clear the area and pack away the decorations. Our three daughters were busy with assigned tasks, when one cried, "Baby Jesus is missing!" While putting away the nativity figurines, she noticed the Christ child was not in Mary's arms.

A frantic search began, with everyone shaking wadded papers, looking for the swaddled Christ child. When the baby figurine fell out of some crumpled tissue, we were happy that the lost was found. Our youngest said, "Now he is safe, and we can put him away until next year."

Later, as I stood looking out the window at the Christmas lights God put in the sky, I was overtaken by a sense of shame and remorse. How is it that we celebrate Christmas, Jesus' birthday, but *miss* Him, the Light of the world, for whom the celebration was made? We enjoy all the trappings— food, decorations, and gifts, but in the bustle we misplace the greatest gift. And, even if we give cursory notice to the Christ child, we pack Him away into the "Christmas Closet" of our lives, ready to bring Him out as a "decoration" for *our* party next year.

I asked God to forgive us for making Christmas more about us than about Christ. I prayed we'd remember whose birthday it is and celebrate its meaning for us on each future Christmas and every day.

Do you struggle with being caught up in the "trappings" of Christmas? If so, what can you do to refocus on making Jesus the center of the celebration?

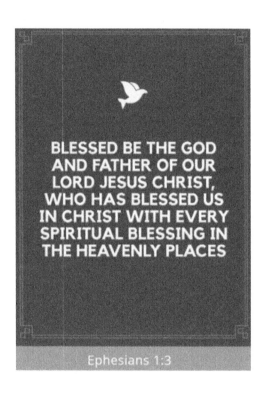

BLESSED BE THE GOD
AND FATHER OF OUR
LORD JESUS CHRIST,
WHO HAS BLESSED US
IN CHRIST WITH EVERY
SPIRITUAL BLESSING IN
THE HEAVENLY PLACES

Ephesians 1:3

"Forever Gifts"

Blessed be the God and Father of our Lord Jesus Christ, who has blessed us in Christ with every spiritual blessing in the heavenly places.
~ Ephesians 1:3

God calls us Christians to be thankful for our blessings. If we were to make a list, we might count material things, such as health, family, basic provisions (housing, clothing, food), and modern conveniences. We could add others that are immaterial, depending on where we live—freedoms, rights, and privileges as citizens, for example.

No matter how long this list might be—none of these blessings lasts. In time, our health deteriorates, death separates us from loved ones, and our basic provisions rot, fade, or turn to dust. Even modern conveniences end up in the trash and immaterial blessings have no guarantees. What gifts are forever? Paul tells us that we have "every spiritual blessing" in Christ. (Ephesians 2:3) In the subsequent verses he lists them:

- We are chosen (v.4)
- We are adopted through Jesus Christ (v.5)
- We are blessed with His grace (v.6)
- We are redeemed through Christ's blood (v.7)
- God has "lavished" wisdom and insight upon us making known the mystery of His will; we are part of His plan through Christ to unite all things in heaven and on earth (v.8-10)
- We are heirs according to the counsel of His will (v.11)
- We are in Christ the praise of His glory (v.12)
- We have the word of truth, the gospel of salvation (v.13a)
- We are sealed with the promised Holy Spirit, the guarantee of our inheritance (v.13b-14)

We have countless blessings during our lives on earth, and we have spiritual blessings in heavenly places to enjoy forever.

Do you thank God for *all* your blessings, including spiritual ones?

Afterword

Thanks for reading *My Faithbook Messages*. God is sending messages to all of us and these are some He has graciously sent to me. I am privileged to share them with you. By the time you read this, I am confident He is continuing to send messages to me and to you.

If you have received messages that resonate with His Faithbook and would like to share them with me, please email them to me at safischer37@gmail.com. I would love to read them.

If you would like to share any of the devotional posts in *My Faithbook Messages*, please refer to the directions on page 124.

Acknowledgements

I am blessed to have my most gracious husband, Craig, who gave me space and time to write.

I'm grateful for my colleagues in the diverse Sandhills Writers Group, Pinehurst, NC who were sounding boards for my work and gave me helpful critiques and encouragement along the way.

Michael Edwards of Faithwriters.com instilled confidence in me by his supportive comments on my devotional submissions.

I appreciate my close friend, Joan Silvestri, who proofread the work with her "eagle" eye to catch pesky errors missed by edits.

Rachel Greene worked her amazing formatting skills with patience and diligence as she did for my first book, "Seasons in the Garden." The result is another beautiful rendition of my work for the good pleasure of my readers.

I am grateful to many family members and friends who gave me support. No writer I know can produce work without the encouragement of such people.

Finally, I could not possibly share any of these devotions without the express grace given me by God through Jesus Christ and the Holy Spirit.

How to Share *My Faithbook Messages*

Any of *My Faithbook Messages* are free to share by email simply upon request. Each message will be formatted with a decorative border, suitable for printing by the recipient.

Here's how to share a Message:

Choose the Faithbook Message you wish to share and use one of two methods below to send it to someone:

- Method #1: If you wish to forward the Message yourself, simply put the title of the Message in the subject line and your name and email address in the body of an email to me: safischer37@gmail.com. I will send a copy directly to you so you can forward it.

- Method #2: If you want me to forward the Message, then follow this procedure:

  Copy or write this into the body of an email to me:

Please send (Title of Devotional) to: (Recipient's name and email address).

(Additional message from you, if you have one)

_____

Your name_____

Your email address_____

Email to me: safischer37@gmail.com

I will send you a carbon copy of the email when I send the Faithbook Message to your recipient.

Thanks for sharing a Faithbook Message!

About the Author

Sandra Fischer taught high school English and owned a Christian bookstore in Indiana before retiring to Dataw Island, South Carolina in 2001. Her writing is devoted to stories gleaned from her experiences growing up in the Midwest and new ones as a Southern transplant. Her book, "Seasons in the Garden" is a collection of prose and poetry, inspired by nature and her association with the Dataw Garden Club. She is published in several anthologies listed on her Amazon author page, and she is a platinum member of Faithwriters.com. After living in South Carolina for 15 years, Sandra relocated to Southern Pines, North Carolina, where she continues to write inspirational articles and create new stories. Follow her at these links:

http://www.faithwriters.com/member-profile.php?id=1729
http://fisch-lines.blogspot.com/
http://www.amazon.com/Sandra-Fischer/e/B00ISC2GA4/
www.sandifischer.com (website coming soon)

Made in the USA
Monee, IL
14 February 2021

59541742R00075